The Gifted and Talented Students in Canada

RESULTS OF A CEA SURVEY

Burton Borthwick, Ian Dow, Denis Lévesque, Ruth Banks

THE CANADIAN EDUCATION ASSOCIATION
L'ASSOCIATION CANADIENNE D'ÉDUCATION
252 Bloor Street West, Suite S850, Toronto, Ontario M5S 1V5

Price: $5.00

1980

Cover: design by Fred Huffman; illustration by Joan Sirr

© THE CANADIAN EDUCATION ASSOCIATION 1980
ISBN 0-919078-65-6

Printed in Canada by
TWIN OFFSET LIMITED

Contents

Photo Credits 6

Acknowledgements 7

The Authors 8

Introduction 9

Part I: Concerns, Issues, and Program Suggestions

How Do You Recognize the Gifted/Talented Students? 15

    DEFINITIONS 15

    IDENTIFICATION OF GIFTED AND TALENTED STUDENTS 16

Misconceptions about the Gifted/Talented 21

    SOCIAL ADJUSTMENT 21

    PERSONALITY 22

    EMOTIONAL STABILITY 23

    PHYSICAL CHARACTERISTICS 23

    MECHANICAL ABILITY 23

Program Organization for the Gifted/Talented Student 25
    SPECIAL SCHOOLS AND SPECIAL CLASSES 26

    ABILITY GROUPING 27

    ACCELERATION 27

    ENRICHMENT 28

    INDEPENDENT STUDY 29

Program Suggestions for the Classroom 31
    GENERAL 31

    TEACHER STRATEGIES 32

Part II: The Triple Survey

Survey of Departments/Ministries of Education 37
    POLICY 37

    LEGISLATION 39

    FUNDING 41

    TRANSPORTATION 42

    TEACHER EDUCATION 43

    RESEARCH AND EVALUATION 45

    CURRICULUM 46

    ASSOCIATIONS 47

Survey of Faculties of Education 49
    TEACHER PREPARATION PROGRAMS 49

    GRADUATE PROGRAMS 50

    PROFESSIONAL DEVELOPMENT ACTIVITIES 50

    GENERAL OBSERVATIONS 51

Survey of School Boards 53
RESULTS OF THE SURVEY 54

Appendixes

A. Works Cited 71

B. Individual Responses from Universities 73

C. School Boards that Submitted Supplementary Material 77

D. Suggested Canadian Reading 79

Photo Credits

The CEA wishes to thank the following for supplying the photographs shown on the pages listed after their names:

RUTH BANKS, 11, 12, 34, 60

JON EASTON, 6, 20, 24, 30, 48, 52, 66

Acknowledgements

In the fall of 1977 the CEA sponsored two regional seminars on "Helping the Gifted: An Investment for the Future", one in Toronto for educators from the Atlantic provinces, Québec, and Ontario, and one in Regina for the western provinces. The experts who acted as the main resource persons for both seminars were Mr. D.T.E. Marjoram, one of Her Majesty's Inspectors with the Department of Education and Science in Britain, a leader in the development and implementation of programs for the gifted for many years, and Dr. Burton Borthwick, at that time an Education Officer in the Special Education Branch of the Ontario Ministry of Education.

During the seminars, it became apparent that there was very little known about the status of education for the gifted and talented in the various regions of Canada. Consequently, a team of educators knowledgeable in this field, coordinated by Burt Borthwick and including Mrs. Ruth Banks of the Scarborough Board of Education (a member of the local arrangements committee for the Toronto seminar) and Drs. Ian Dow and Denis Lévesque of the University of Ottawa, offered to conduct a survey under the sponsorship of the CEA in the fall and winter of 1978-79. The present report is the happy result of this joint enterprise.

The authors (and the CEA) express their gratitude to personnel in the provincial departments and ministries of education, university faculties of education, and school boards who responded to the questionnaires used for the survey.

The assistance of numerous other persons who provided additional material for the report is also acknowledged. The material received and the comments submitted have been constructive and helpful.

Gerald N. Nason
Executive Director
Canadian Education Association

The Authors

Dr. Burton L. Borthwick is the Program Director of Trillium School in Milton, Ontario (Canada's first government-funded residential school for children with learning disabilities), and a former Education Officer in the Special Education Branch of the Ontario Ministry of Education.

Dr. Ian I. Dow is an Associate Professor in the Department of Educational Studies of the Faculty of Education of the University of Ottawa. Dr. Dow was involved with a gifted child program while employed as a principal with the Ottawa Board of Education.

Dr. Denis R. Lévesque is an Assistant Professor in the Teacher Education Department of the Faculty of Education of the University of Ottawa.

Mrs. Ruth G. Banks is the Supervisor of Gifted Programs at the Scarborough (Ontario) Board of Education. Mrs. Banks is also the principal of Churchill Heights, a junior kindergarten to grade 6 public school in which many of the gifted children who come under the jurisdiction of Scarborough Board are housed. As this report goes to press, about 28% of the students at Churchill Heights have been identified as gifted.

Introduction

It was the second day of school and the grade 2 children stared openly at a newcomer: six-year-old Charlie who had been moved abruptly into their room after one day in grade 1. Charlie stared back and wasn't happy with what he saw: the childish handwriting of two students close to him; the clumsy attempt by a boy a head taller than he to solve an easy arithmetic question.

Charlie tried to relax by concentrating on his stamp collection at home, remembering his lengthy correspondence battle the previous year with one company. (Dear Sir: I plan to take you to court unless your nuisance bills stop immediately for stamps that I have not ordered. I am five years old.) Just then, the teacher picked up something from the floor. "Who dropped an eraser?" Charlie tried to stifle a giggle. The teacher, reddening, demanded to know the joke. The new boy looked around the class and again giggled: "Who shaves around here?"

It happened just that way. Six-year-old Charlie, elevated from grade 1 after a day that one teacher will never forget, had taught himself to read at the age of three and to type at the age of four. He was reading Shakespeare for pleasure a year later, and at six had a complete grasp of world geography because of his bulging stamp collection. As his teacher discovered, he also found humour in puns that went over the heads of all his classmates — and sometimes the teacher too.

Pity the teacher. But also pity the gifted student.

For too long, the gifted or talented student has not had an easy time in the average Canadian classroom. Sputnik prompted a flurry of interest in this student in the late 1950s — particularly in the student gifted in the area of science — but the resulting expansion in programs for the gifted didn't last. Other needs in education crowded to the fore, such as the need for more vocational training, and education for the gifted was somewhat neglected.

However, this publication bears cheering evidence of changing circumstances in special education for our gifted and talented students. A cross-Canada survey, undertaken by the authors and sponsored by the Canadian Education Association in the fall and winter of 1978-79, discovered, for example, that one out of every three responding school boards was either conducting or planning a pilot project for its gifted and talented students. And, almost everywhere, the survey found an avid curiosity about the latest research data in this field. Results of that survey are reported for the first time publicly in these pages.

Anyone who has taken some interest in educational journals in the last half-dozen years has witnessed an outbreak of articles that seek to explain why the gifted student has had a low priority.

Many reasons are cited. There is the traditional peer pressure which tells a gifted student not to appear to be different. But on top of that, many communities have seemed downright hostile to the concept of special education for the gifted ("they'll get along well anyway"); the regular school curriculum creates the impression that a gifted student is performing well because he or she is receiving better than average marks, while in reality the student is working far below his/her potential; and, as many researchers have found, the gifted student often confuses the situation by "turning off". (A U.S. researcher has said that fewer than half of the male students in the top 30% of academic ability graduated from college; the percentage was far worse for gifted female students.)[1]

In 1971, one writer-researcher thought the pendulum had swung far enough that gifted students should be protected by their own Bill of Rights. Norman Mirman wrote in the *Gifted Child Quarterly:*

"I think we need to recognize that under the present system of education, gifted students are subtle targets of discrimination through negative factors engaged by attentiveness to anti-poverty, anti-dropout, and other legitimate priorities, by misguided or overt attempts by teachers to level or equalize performance, and by the negative attitudes of peer groups toward scholastic excellence. We must further recognize that the present attitude of the community, parents, and even professional educators is not only indifferent, but frequently quite hostile to the idea of special education for the gifted. . . . The gifted child is frequently the most *neglected* student in our educational programming. The regular school curriculum only barely approximates the demands of either the greater learning capacity or the anticipated social roles of the gifted."[2]

Strong words. But proof that they are being heard is the fact that the U.S. Department of Education has established an office for the gifted and talented. In Canada, provincial departments/ministries of education are encouraging local school boards to develop programs for gifted and talented students. It is very significant that, in a time of shrinking educational resources, local school boards in Canada are making efforts to end the neglect of their ablest students. More than anything else, the changing attitudes of school boards must be the true indicator of community opinion about programming for this exceptional group.

As this report indicates, there has been some confusion over the definition of a gifted or talented student. You will find the most recent research summarized in the next chapter.

The survey results that appear later in this report offer a rare perspective on how several levels of education in Canada approach a specific need.

---

[1]Donald S. Bridgman, as quoted in Dael Wolfle, "Diversity of Talent", in J.L. French (ed.), *Educating the Gifted,* rev. ed. (New York: Holt, Rinehart and Winston, 1964), p. 25.

[2]Norman Mirman, "Education of the Gifted in the 70s", *The Gifted Child Quarterly,* Vol. 15, No. 3 (Autumn 1971), p. 218.

- Provincial departments/ministries of education were asked to define their approaches to special education for gifted and talented students in terms of policy, legislation, funding, teacher training, and research. Their responses are reprinted with as little editing as possible.
- Twenty-one universities answered a questionnaire that was sent to every faculty of education in Canada. The remarkably high return represents all ten provinces and includes both large and small institutions.
- The strong response from school boards, including the many requests for more information about what others were doing, provides a clear indicator that community attitudes towards special education for the gifted or talented student are changing in Canada.

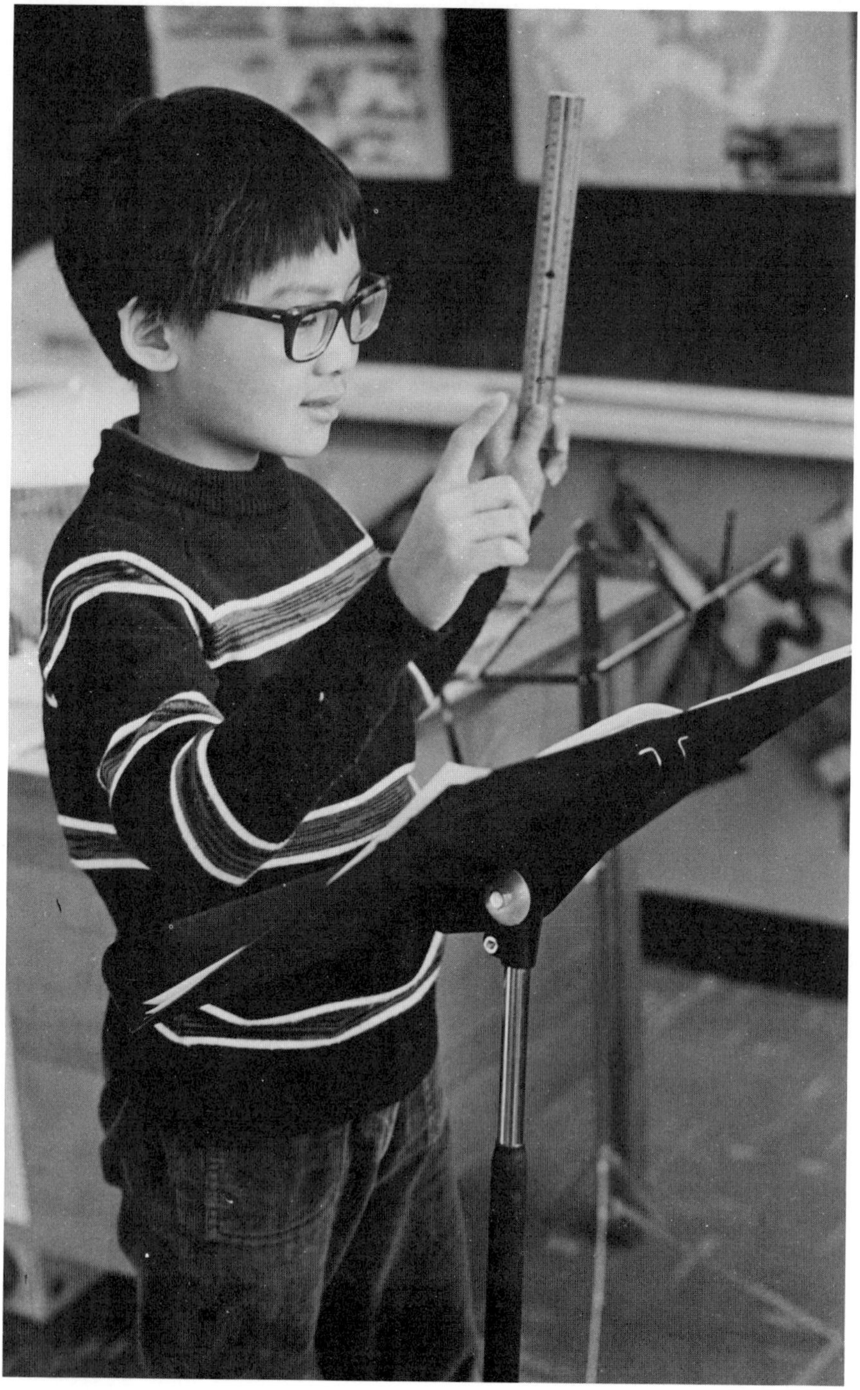

Part I: Concerns, Issues, and Program Suggestions

How Do You Recognize the Gifted/Talented Students?

One of Albert Einstein's first teachers thought he'd have difficulty learning to read. Winston Churchill was considered to be dull-normal at best—even by his own father.

History is filled with so many similar cases that it's small wonder the issue of how to decide who's gifted and who's not is still hotly debated. Different school jurisdictions across Canada use different ways of measuring talent or intellectual ability, as the CEA survey confirms.

Here is a look at what current research has to say about the sensitive question of identifying gifted and talented students in the classroom.

DEFINITIONS

The literature indicates that there are a number of definitions for this group of students. Some refer only to the gifted, others only to the talented, with recent definitions combining the two aspects.

There appear to be three types of definitions: objective, descriptive, and comparative.

Objective definitions of gifted or talented students are concerned with scores or measures on intellectual or aptitude tests. Lewis Terman's research dealt with a population having an intellectual score of at least 140 on the Stanford-Binet Intelligence Test, whereas Leta Hollingworth defined her population as those with an intellective functioning of 130 and above.[3] Some school boards still rely on an objective definition for selecting students for their gifted programs.

Descriptive definitions give the characteristics of gifted and talented people. Often a test consisting of a check list is used for this purpose. *Project Equity*, a report published by the Carleton Board of Education, indicates that descriptive definitions emphasize "achievement, extraordinary curiosity, creative thinking, unusual ability to understand abstractions, exceptional breadth of interest, artistic ability and even advanced physical and social maturity".[4]

---

[3]References to the research of Terman and Hollingworth on the social adjustment of gifted children appear in the next chapter. It was Terman who devised the Stanford-Binet Intelligence Test, the first widely used I.Q. test in the U.S.

[4]*Project Equity* (Ottawa: Carleton Board of Education, 1973), p. 118.

Comparative definitions single out those students who demonstrate superior academic achievement compared to the majority.

The U.S. Department of Education and the Province of Ontario have accepted definitions that contain aspects of all three types.

According to the U.S. Department of Education:

"Gifted and talented children are those identified by professionally qualified persons who, by virtue of outstanding abilities, are capable of high performance. These are children who require differentiated educational programs and/or services beyond those normally provided by the regular school program in order to realize their contribution to self and society."[5]

The Province of Ontario has accepted the term gifted as one that

"refers to pupils of a superior degree of general intellectual ability. Such pupils are so advanced of the regular class population that they require special provisions beyond the normal program. The term 'talented' refers to those pupils who excel in an area such as music, visual arts, drama, athletics, or in specific academic areas. Gifted/talented children may be identified within one of the following groups:

- intellectual — academically outstanding
- aesthetic — outstanding in the creative arts
- kinesthetic — outstanding in coordination and motor abilities
- psycho-social — outstanding in human relations and leadership ability"[6]

In spite of the differences noted in the defintions reported in the literature, each refers to 2 to 3% of the population.

IDENTIFICATION OF GIFTED AND TALENTED STUDENTS

Identification of the gifted and talented appears to be complicated by extreme diversity of viewpoint both on how to do it and on precisely what differentiates the gifted or talented from bright children. In the past, gifted children were identified according to their intellectual functioning. If a student acquired a score of 130 or 140 $\pm$ on a Stanford-Binet or WISC[7] test, he or she was considered gifted. Today, educators are beginning to question the validity of such tests and are recognizing the complexity of identifying this group of students.

Identification of the gifted and talented should be done as a series of steps followed by specific plans for programming. The first step is to select candidates through the use of multiple methods, such as group intelligence and achievement tests, teacher nominations, parent

---

[5]U.S. Office of Education, *Education of the Gifted and Talented,* Vol. 1: *Report to the Congress of the United States by the U.S. Commissioner of Education* (Washington, D.C.: Washington Monitoring Service by the Editors of *Education U.S.A.,* 1971), p. 5.

[6]*Gifted/Talented Children,* Curriculum Ideas for Teachers (Toronto: Ontario Ministry of Education, 1978), p. 2.

[7]Wechsler Intelligence Scale for Children.

interviews, and consideration of past achievement. The second step is an individualized assessment.

Giftedness in children is not easily recognized. All the attributes or facets of giftedness seldom or never appear in total in any one child. Moreover, the patterns or combinations of patterns of aptitudes, skills, or abilities that make up giftedness are many and varied. Potentialities may exist but not be realized.

There are many factors that educators should consider when developing a selection procedure.

Firstly, tests have limitations in identifying students, in that the standardized tests most often used in the selection process measure the types of thought processes considered acceptable in the academic area. The creative, divergent thinker does not do well on such tests.

Secondly, children from minority groups are forced to compete on unequal terms with white, middle class children. In *Psychological Testing of American Minorities: Issues and Consequences,* Ronald Samuda states:

"Aside from postulating a normal distribution of the population, standardization procedures have also been based on the assumption that the white middle class standards, values, attitudes, beliefs, experiences, and knowledge are the only correct ones, thereby denying minority groups and poor whites the recognition of their cultural distinctiveness."[8]

Thirdly, underachievement begins to manifest itself as early as five years of age. The underachiever often becomes frustrated and consequently a behaviour problem, and reacts negatively, resulting in parental anxiety and frequently conflict in the home. Parents describe such children as early achievers, as being expert or having interest in a single area, such as science or math. They also describe them as attention seekers and hyperactive in the home environment. J. Whitmore's study indicates that 90% of gifted underachieving children are males.[9] Teachers report that such children display day-dreaming, disruptive behaviour; they are easily distracted and have unhealthy self-concepts.

The following are indicators of the gifted underachiever that may assist one in making an identification:

1. Superior verbal performance—advanced vocabulary and concepts.
2. Exceptional fund of knowledge—usually an "expert" in one particular area.
3. Superior retention, but will do little written work to reinforce concepts.
4. Creative, inventive.
5. Self-critical; a perfectionist who rarely meets his/her goals.
6. Perceptive and sensitive to situations seemingly beyond his/her years.
7. Poor self-concept; often frustrated.
8. An I.Q. score in the very superior range.

---

[8]Ronald J. Samuda, *Psychological Testing of American Minorities: Issues and Consequences* (New York: Dodd, Mead, 1975), p. 7.

[9]J. Whitmore, *The Gifted Underachiever* (Nashville, Tenn.: Geo. Peabody College for Teachers).

The teacher often becomes frustrated in attempting to meet the needs of the underachiever, as this child is not motivated by the usual stimuli to learning. It is important for the teacher to develop in the underachieving child a sense of self-worth and to create a learning environment where failure and rejection are minimal.

Here are brief descriptions of some of the tests and procedures used in Canada to select gifted and talented students.

Teacher Nomination

Nomination by teachers is one of the most widely used and recommended means for identifying potentially gifted pupils, yet the method is of limited usefulness. Studies show that alone, teacher nomination proves the least effective screen. However, other studies indicate that when the judgement of teachers is combined with rating scales based on lists of characteristics of giftedness, the likelihood that children will not be overlooked for referral is increased.

It is generally agreed that rating scales are useful in identifying giftedness, but they should be used with full awareness of their limitations. If scales are adapted or developed for local use, they should consist of items that are clearly understood by teachers and include those qualities or traits which are readily identified in classroom situations. Items based on direct observation of behaviour are far more valuable than those based on inference.

Nomination by Others

An open opportunity to nominate a student as gifted should be given to all those who are in a position to know his/her high capabilities: former teachers, principals, other school resource personnel, parents, peers, and community members. Often school personnel other than the current teacher have had numerous contacts with a child and have formed accurate opinions of his/her ability.

Group Intelligence, Achievement, and Creativity Tests

These tests are helpful in screening for gifted pupils, especially if used together. But group tests should be employed for screening purposes only, not for final identification. The drawback to using group tests to identify the gifted is that their content is designed for the majority of pupils within certain age and grade ranges; content suitable for the gifted is limited to a few items. Because there is such a small number of advanced items, pupils must have nearly total success to be designated as gifted. The problem that results from using group tests is that an artificial "ceiling" or limit is imposed on a child's I.Q. score. Studies show that the ceiling may cause a child's I.Q. to vary 30 points from an individual to a group test, especially at the upper levels of measured intellectual ability.

Nevertheless, used in combination with other methods, group tests are effective screening devices. They are relatively inexpensive; but it should be kept in mind that they fail to identify some gifted students and they sometimes identify erroneously.

Individual Tests of Intelligence

Individual intelligence tests have a number of advantages over group tests. A broader sampling of abilities is possible, better testing conditions can be arranged, a greater range of aptitude in any area can be tested, and an interpretation of the quality of performance is possible.

Obvious problems include the cost, lack of trained test administrators, and some content in the tests which penalizes children with language or environmental handicaps. Individual intelligence tests have also been criticized for their inadequacy in identifying creative potential and a number of traits important to success, such as values, habits, and perseverance.

Studies have shown that while the individual intelligence tests do not measure all human abilities, they do identify gifted children much more effectively than group measures. It is important to use an individual test that provides an adequate ceiling and measurement of a number of abilities. The Stanford-Binet and the Wechsler Intelligence Scale for Children are the two full-length individual tests in widespread use for testing the gifted. They have been compared by a number of authorities who believe that the Stanford-Binet is more suitable for this purpose. The Binet has a higher I.Q. range than the WISC, and some studies show that I.Q.s of gifted children average about ten points lower on the full-scale WISC than they do on the Binet.

The Case Study

The end product of the identification process is a case study where all information concerning a student and his/her unique abilities, talents, interests, psychological traits, and specific educational accomplishments and needs are made apparent to educators. In the study, consideration should be given to the child's health, language status, intellectual stimulation at home, possibility for study at home, nutrition, attitudes of parents and peers and teachers toward learning and achievement, attitudes of teachers toward the child and his/her potential for learning, and the child's opportunities for success. The more complete the information, the greater the base for understanding and effective planning.

The study should be cumulative. Often the child can contribute an autobiography, or a list of interests or products.

A case study of the gifted can be relatively inexpensive, and it takes comparatively little time to do.

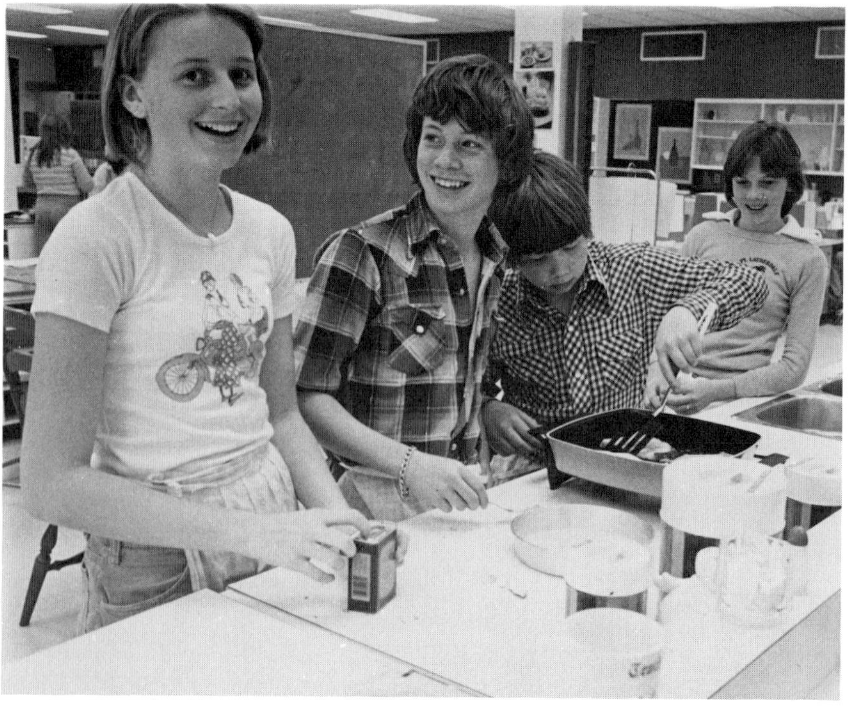

Misconceptions about the Gifted/Talented

Without reading the caption, you instantly recognize the child genius in a cartoon: smaller than the other children, wearing thick glasses that look far too big for the babyish face, always with a heavy book under one arm.

If you believe writers or poets from the past, that child misfit will probably grow up to be not quite all there, perhaps mad. Seneca, who died in A.D. 65, summed it up: "There is no great genius without some touch of madness."

We smile at the obvious distortions, but far too many adults still have misconceptions and prejudices about gifted or talented students. Teachers should be aware of the misconceptions and have a clear basic understanding of the individual differences exhibited by gifted and talented children before teaching them or developing curricula for them.

SOCIAL ADJUSTMENT

Many people believe that there is a tendency for gifted children to be socially maladjusted. However, there is sufficient evidence to contradict this belief. In Lewis Terman's study of 1921-22, 84% of the gifted group were rated as equal or above the mean of the unselected group in social interest and adjustment. Terman also indicated that even though the gifted child was usually younger than the average age of his/her classmates, he/she had approximately the same number of school friends as the other children.[10]

If one bases the evidence of social adjustment on participation in the various extracurricular activities, then the gifted child is better socially adjusted than the average.

In 1938, Noel Keys reported that the underage high school student equalled or surpassed the control group with respect to participation in student activities. He also found that bright pupils who had accelerated from two to five semesters were better socially adjusted than those who remained at their grade according to their chronological age.[11]

Similar findings were reported by Edna Lamson. In her study, the gifted group exceeded the control group in participation in extracurricular

---

[10] M.R. Sumption and E.M. Luecking, *Education of the Gifted* (New York: Ronald Press, 1960), p. 83.

[11] Ibid., pp. 83-84.

activities by approximately 25%. She concluded that the young gifted were not discouraged from participation because of immaturity.[12]

Terman re-evaluated his gifted group in 1940 when they were in college. He found that the gifted, on the whole, participated to a greater extent in extracurricular activities than the normal college population.[13]

There seems to be sufficient evidence in the literature to indicate that gifted children and college students have little difficulty in social adjustment. However, the extremely gifted child may have more trouble adjusting to the social norms than the typical gifted person. The extremely gifted child has interests that differ greatly from those of the average child. He or she is somewhat isolated, in that statistically there are fewer children with exceptionally high intelligence; therefore, the extremely gifted child has few playmates of the same intellectual potential. However, in a group of gifted children he/she is likely to be more socially accepted than in a group of average children. Also, in the gifted group the extremely gifted child is apt to achieve the role of leader.

Leta Hollingworth reported that the leader of a group is likely to be more intelligent, but not too much more intelligent, than the average of the group. The higher the I.Q., the less chance there is of being leader of an average group. However, in a group with above-average intelligence, the extremely gifted child may very well be the popular leader.[14]

The I.Q. is not the only determinant variable in becoming the leader of the group. Some gifted children or adults have personality traits that would make them favourites with associates of any age, whether of average or below-average intelligence. Other gifted people have personality traits that limit their chance of being a leader in almost any group. However, on the whole the gifted possess those qualities that lend to leadership ability.

PERSONALITY

According to K.C. Garrison and D.G. Force, "Historically, there has been a rather common notion that most geniuses are 'freaks' or are unstable in nature"; however, they go on to indicate that the work of Lewis Terman and his collaborators has provided sufficient evidence to support the conclusion that intellectual precocity is not in any manner associated with antisocial or undesirable personalities. Analysis of the studies indicates that the personality traits of gifted children tend to be more desirable than the personality traits of average children of the same age.[15] Elsewhere in research the conclusion has been reached that the

---

[12]Edna E.A. Lamson, *A Study of Young Gifted Children in Senior High School,* Contributions to Education No. 424 (New York: Bureau of Publications, Teachers College, Columbia University, 1930), p. 74.

[13]L.M. Terman and M.H. Oden, *The Gifted Child Grows Up: Twenty-five Year Follow-up of a Superior Group,* Genetic Studies of Genius, Vol. IV (Stanford, Calif.: Stanford University Press, 1947), p. 97.

[14]Leta S. Hollingworth, *Gifted Children: Their Nature and Nurture* (New York: The Macmillan Co., 1926), p. 131.

[15]K.C. Garrison and D.G. Force, *The Psychology of Exceptional Children,* 4th ed. (New York: Ronald Press, 1965), p. 134.

gifted as a group are humorous and playful, have "off the beaten track" ideas, are conscientious, truthful, courteous, and cooperative, and demonstrate independence and forcefulness. Thus, according to the standards of our society, the gifted display desirable personalities.

EMOTIONAL STABILITY

The emotional characteristics of the gifted and talented have been stereotyped to some degree by such statements as "genius is akin to madness." Fortunately, it has been demonstrated by many studies that there is no basis in fact for this kind of statement.

Research carried out by Hollingworth, Terman, and others has provided information and conclusions that oppose the view that the gifted are maladjusted. In fact it appears that as a group they have a more wholesome social attitude and are as well-adjusted, if not better, than children of average intelligence.

PHYSICAL CHARACTERISTICS

We referred earlier to the cartoonist's concept of the gifted or the mental prodigy as bifocaled, hollow-chested, and undersized. This is not the case in real life. According to Hollingworth's studies

"It has been amply proved, by measurements, that highly intelligent children are tall, heavy, strong, healthy, and fine looking as a group, exceeding the generality of children in all these respects. This does not mean that every individual among the gifted is physically superior, but it does mean that a gifted child is more likely to have a fine body than is a child taken from the general population."[16]

Hollingworth also indicated that the health history of gifted children compares favourably with that of children of the normal or dull groups. They have fewer physical defects and their mortality rates are lower.[17]

MECHANICAL ABILITY

The gifted more frequently than is assumed illustrate high mechanical performance. Many complicated machines, such as the computer, telephone, and airplane, have been produced by individuals who possess a combination of high mental ability, mechanical ability, and creative imagination.

There is a clear distinction between the gifted whose performance is along mechanical lines and the person who possesses mechanical skills. The person who possesses mechanical skills and has a manipulative skill, and therefore is able to perform complicated mechanical tasks, is not necessarily gifted intellectually. The gifted individual who has a high

---

[16]Sumption and Luecking, op. cit., p. 74.
[17]Ibid., p. 109.

degree of mechanical interest and intellectual ability is able to perform tasks beyond the manipulative stage. This type of gifted individual contributes largely on the theoretical level, providing solutions for mechanical problems and often creating new machines.[18]

Mechanical giftedness is measured by mechanical aptitude tests. These tests gauge the ability to assess spatial relationships, visual perceptions of mechanical patterns, and matching configurations. Probably one of the best indicators of mechanical giftedness in early childhood is the way the child manipulates objects. The gifted child more often than the average creates mechanical devices and manipulates mechanical objects with skill.[19]

---

[18]Ibid., p. 17.
[19]Ibid.

Program Organization for the Gifted/Talented Student

Most educational systems in Canada support the concept that every child has the right to the opportunity to become educated to his or her level of ability.

In order to achieve this goal for gifted and talented students, specialized programs are needed. The research literature indicates conclusively that gifted children do not learn effectively when grouped with children of average ability. If appropriate programs are not provided, the gap between achievement and potential may become wider than it is among average students.[20]

Norman Mirman proposes that the gifted child has the right to expect the school to provide:

"1. An *educational environment* where learning is important and his intellect is respected — not resented or looked down upon.
2. Exposure to large bodies of knowledge.
3. Basic opportunities to interact with teachers who recognize that he sometimes requires more freedom, less control, and time to make discoveries.
4. A climate where a student may discuss, examine, and support a position or a stand without fear of ridicule by his peers or the intervention of personalized teacher value judgements.
5. Opportunities to hear and speak with persons who can act as models — both implicitly and explicitly — who intellectually represent the gifted community.
6. Training in the acquisition of work habits which will contribute to his success in school and in later professional or business activities.
7. Opportunities and encouragement which enhance the development of a positive self-concept."[21]

In order to meet the needs of gifted and talented students, school boards in Canada have developed a variety of program organizational

---

[20] E.L. Horwitz, "Gifted Children", *Children Today*, Vol. 2, No. 1 (Jan.-Feb. 1973), pp. 27-30.

[21] Norman Mirman, "Education of the Gifted in the 70s", *The Gifted Child Quarterly*, Vol. 15, No. 3 (Autumn 1971), pp. 219-221.

patterns, consisting of the following: special schools, special classes, ability grouping, acceleration, Saturday classes, enrichment, and independent study.

SPECIAL SCHOOLS AND SPECIAL CLASSES

In Canada, there are few schools designed specifically for gifted/talented children. However, there are a number of special classes.

The literature indicates the advantages and disadvantages of placing gifted and talented children in homogeneous groups. Some of the advantages are:

— It provides greater opportunities for gifted and talented students to interact with other students of similar intellect and interests. Often such interaction adds stimulus to the learning environment.
— Special classes may be better able to allow students to work at their own speed, within their own abilities, and in their personal areas of interest.
— A teacher can more easily meet the educational needs of gifted and talented students if not held responsible for the teaching of slower students within the same classroom.
— A special class gives gifted and talented students a better perspective on their actual potential; in a regular class such students may not find intellect or talents challenged.
— In a special class, gifted and talented students may have more opportunities to explore their ideas and interests and may receive support and recognition from other students. The research literature indicates that gifted and talented students support each other as they work together.
— A special class approach makes it possible for the school board to hire a teacher specifically qualified to teach this group of students.

There are also some disadvantages in placing gifted and talented students in special schools and classes. Traditionally it has been stated that segregation creates and promotes élitism; that special grouping is undemocratic, in that it extends special privileges and an enriched program to those students who need it least. Some of the disadvantages that have been reported are:

— Segregated programs may promote snobbery among the gifted and talented, who may develop a feeling of superiority and self-importance.
— Such a setting may not provide a realistic environment to prepare gifted/talented students for the everyday world.
— Some educators believe that students in special schools or classes may be under greater pressure to achieve than they would be in a regular classroom. Often standards are higher and competition keener, which may lead to greater expectations of the students.
— Students in the regular classes lose a rich resource and lack stimulation when gifted and talented students are placed in segregated classes.

— Some educators feel that special classes for gifted and talented students cost more money than other types of programs. However, at least one research report indicates that the extra costs are insignificant.[22]

ABILITY GROUPING

Ability grouping or partial withdrawal has been a traditional approach by educators to meeting the needs of gifted and talented students. It may take place within special or regular classrooms, or within a family of schools.

This organizational pattern encourages the grouping of gifted and talented students according to their ability, interest, and level of performance. It accommodates students who are generally gifted as well as those who are gifted or talented in certain areas. Reported as some of the advantages of ability grouping are the following:

— It promotes a greater degree of freedom to encourage creativity and exploration.
— It reduces the range of intellectual and talent diversity in a class and increases the proportion of relevant instruction for each student.
— It encourages the principal to place the most able teacher, one with special skills and knowledge, in charge of a group of children with similar abilities and interests. Such a setting promotes critical thinking and interaction between able minds.
— It encourages a lower teacher-pupil ratio for instruction and allows for greater individualization of programming.
— It allows greater flexibility for scheduling of special events and field studies.
— It creates more opportunities for students to develop leadership ability.

Below are listed some of the disadvantages of ability grouping:

— Additional staff and space may be required; time-tabling and organization could be more complex.
— Care must be taken to ensure that the total program is well balanced, that areas or subjects of less interest to the students are not neglected.
— Evaluation procedures for the total program may be complex and difficult to administer.

ACCELERATION

Basically there are two ways of accelerating students, one being the skipping of grades and the other a form of continuous progress. In recent years educators have favoured the continuous progress approach, which offers the following advantages:

---

[22]Ian Dow and B. Donnelly, "Differentiated Programs for Gifted Intermediate Students" (University of Ottawa/Ontario Ministry of Education, 1977). Unpublished report.

— It allows a student to progress according to ability.
— It can be modified to allow both acceleration and enrichment. That is, a student who has completed the requirement for a course can then take additional courses or study the same one in more depth.
— It is a good guard against boredom and behaviour problems. Gifted students do not have idle time to fill while waiting for their slower peers to progress.
— It allows a student to complete an education in shorter time and begin a career sooner, or possibly to spend a year travelling or exploring an area of interest before entering the work force.

The advantage of skipping grades is that a student can complete his/her education a year or two sooner. The disadvantages of this method of acceleration appear to outweigh the advantage:

— Students who skip grades often miss the fundamentals and sequencing of learning; this may result in difficulty in later studies.
— Students may advance academically well beyond their social and emotional maturity. Most 10- or 11-year-old students would have difficulty adjusting to the social pressure in a secondary school setting. They would have few peers or friends with whom to interact on a social level, and few opportunities to participate in extracurricular and sports activities.
— There is also high probability that a very young student who displays more knowledge than older classmates will be ridiculed and/or become the butt of practical jokes.

ENRICHMENT

Enrichment programs for the gifted and talented are rather varied. Analysis leads one to conclude that there are two basic types; these could be classified as vertical and horizontal. The vertical type allows students to study at a level beyond their grade in a particular subject. The horizontal type advocates study in depth and breadth at the students' ability level. Ideally, enrichment should include elements of both the vertical and horizontal.

Some of the advantages of vertical enrichment are that

— It allows completion of basic education in less time, giving the student more opportunity for specialization in his/her area of interest.
— It negates boredom, allowing more opportunity for challenge.
— It allows secondary school students the opportunity to accumulate credits beyond those that are required. For example, a student in an academic course may wish to acquire technical credits.
— The cost of education is reduced for those who are able to complete the program in fewer years.

However, there are disadvantages to vertical enrichment:

— It tends to accelerate some students more rapidly than their physical and emotional growth can accommodate.

— There is a possible danger that gaps in learning may occur as a result of too-rapid progress.

Horizontal enrichment has the advantage of allowing students to study and master an area of interest. But it, too, has disadvantages:

— There is a danger of students specializing too early and foregoing the asset of a broad base for their learning.
— The possibility exists of enriching students horizontally at the expense of vertical progress.

INDEPENDENT STUDY

Independent study is an individualized program designed to meet the needs of gifted or talented students who have displayed an ability to study on their own under the direction or guidance of a teacher or monitor. It may be conducted within the regular school facility, a university setting, or the community. Most independent studies involve a number of resource people who have specific knowledge and skills.

Independent studies should be well organized and demand the same standards as other programs for gifted and talented students. According to *Project Equity*, the individual learner should be permitted repeated opportunities to make creative responses within the context of meaningful tasks — to generate his/her own questions and ideas, to follow up intuitive hunches, to develop and pursue his/her own plan of attack on a problem. The primary purpose in giving direction to the student's effort should not be the singling out of one correct response, but rather the encouragement of a range or diversity of responses, a kind of creative feedback that is reinforcing for all children, regardless of the particular responses given.[23]

Some of the advantages of independent study appear to be that

— It provides an opportunity for a student to probe deeply and intensively into an area of specific interest.
— It promotes the ability of a student to work on his/her own and increases research skills.
— It allows a teacher to expand the total school program for gifted and talented students.

There are also some disadvantages to independent study:

— Some students do not function well under limited supervision.
— In most cases such a program is only suitable for older students who are able to be responsible for their own transportation to and from the various learning facilities within the community.
— The success of independent study may be difficult to evaluate. To ensure that adequate evaluation is made, evaluation procedures should be part of the program.

---

[23]*Project Equity* (Ottawa: Carleton Board of Education, 1973), p. 130.

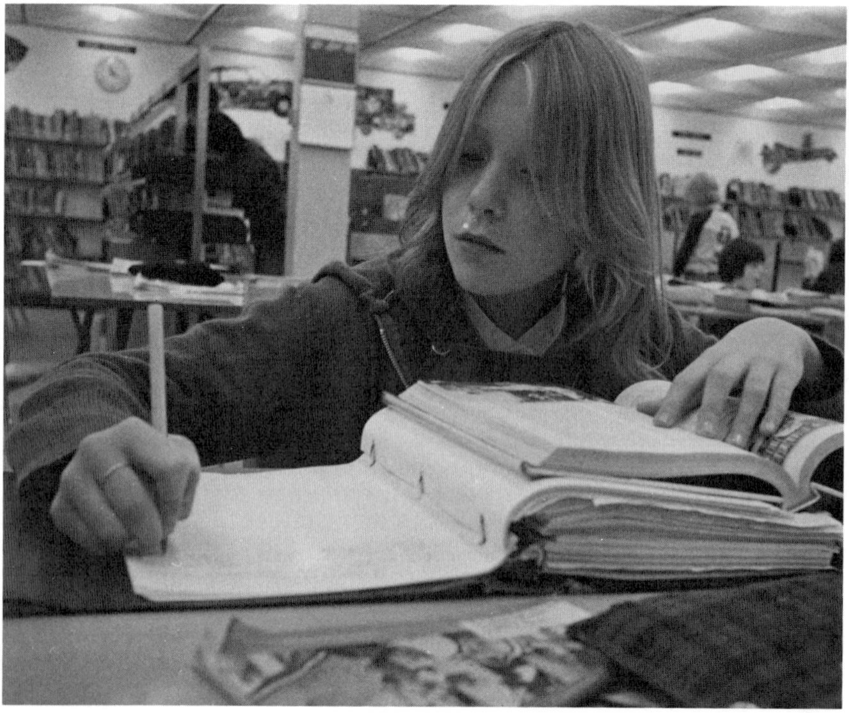

Program Suggestions for the Classroom

Quite obviously, the teacher's role in helping the gifted and talented to realize their potential is a most important and demanding one. With the assistance of support staff, courses of study should be modified to meet the needs of these exceptional children and resources located for the modified courses. The following suggestions are offered in the hope that they will be of some help in performing this heavy but ultimately rewarding task.

GENERAL

A. To instil basic skills commensurate with the pupil's ability, the program should
   — allow for the learning of research skills at an early age;
   — meet the needs of superior mental ability for advanced knowledge acquisition in a short period of time;
   — allow for high intellectual skill development in analysing, synthesizing, and evaluating;
   — encourage divergent thinking;
   — make optimum use of materials and human resources;
   — individualize learning through behavioural objectives and contracts for independent study;
   — continuously evaluate pupil progress and program effectiveness.

B. To develop confidence and a feeling of self-worth in the pupils, the successful program
   — encourages them to work at appropriate levels of difficulty;
   — requires them to evaluate their own tasks;
   — invites them to pursue studies and activities that interest them;
   — fosters pride in tasks well done.

C. In order for the pupils to acquire knowledge and attitudes that will encourage their active participation in Canadian society, the program should stimulate
   — respect for the opinions of others;
   — evaluative thinking;
   — discussions of leadership and the acquisition of knowledge about great Canadian leaders;

- an interest in Canadian history and in experiences relevant to the Canadian mosaic;
- an appreciation and understanding of the contribution that many cultural groups make to Canadian society.

D. To develop moral and aesthetic sensitivity in the children, the program should allow
   - open discussion of moral issues;
   - the development of a sense of humour;
   - opportunities to appreciate the aesthetic aspects of life.

E. Programs for gifted pupils must
   - consider pupils' interests;
   - match their learning style and rate;
   - be oriented to the process of thinking rather than to content.

TEACHER STRATEGIES

In developing a program, the teacher might wish to consult the *Taxonomy of Educational Objectives: Cognitive and Affective Domains* by Benjamin S. Bloom et al. (New York: David McKay, 1960; distributed in Canada by Academic Press, Don Mills, Ont.), *The Structure of Intellect Model: Its Uses and Implications* by J.P. Guilford and P.R. Merrifield (Los Angeles: University of Southern California, 1960), or *Structure of Intellect: Its Interpretation and Uses* by Mary Nacol Meeker (Columbus, Ohio: Charles E. Merrill, 1969; distributed in Canada by Charles E. Merrill, Weston, Ont., a division of Bell & Howell). These books stress processes of thinking and include material that can be used as patterns in developing curricula.

In order to incorporate higher-level thinking into the learning process, certain strategies should be introduced as early as possible:

Research — The skills and habits of independent work that are essential to research can be fostered as early as grade 1. Such skills include using time wisely, knowing how to search for required information, reading critically, taking notes, and remembering facts.

Creative Problem-Solving — A problem-solving approach to learning allows the teacher to give the children much guidance and practice in research activities. The teacher should help the child to tackle a problem in an organized fashion: to clarify it, decide on a method of procedure, research and collect data, keep an open mind, think of many ideas, check opinions against facts.

Interest Centres

The development of an interest centre can be a highly creative endeavour. The most important requirements for its success are that it contain dynamic material with the power to stimulate children to further research and that ample time be allowed for browsing and exploring.

The teacher should not impose teacher-designed projects, but should allow the product of research to be the result of the special investigation and interest of the pupils. Above all, the teacher should avoid asking for a "report", which is frequently a mere recapitulation of existing material. Although a great deal of freedom is allowed, pupils should be aware that activities must be pursued purposefully.

The selection of appropriate material for the centre is crucial, because the objective is not simply to provide information but to provoke curiosity that will lead to further research. Material should include descriptive information of a general rather than of a specific nature. The objective here is to encourage exploration in new areas of potential interest.

Brainstorming

The following procedure is recommended:
— The rule is set down that no criticism of any idea is to be given; the more ideas there are, the better.
— List the ideas given by the pupils.
— Make a general grouping of ideas.
— List topics and headings.
— Condense the ideas and place them under appropriate headings.

Stimulating Sensitivity to Problems

In an activity similar to those suggested for divergent thinking, children should be asked to discuss such questions as what would happen if everyone in the world became deaf, or if we all had only three fingers, or if someone invented a pill as a substitute for all food.

Seminars

Seminars are proving to be worthwhile modes of learning for gifted/talented pupils in later grades. Problem-solving is emphasized.

Self-initiated Learning

This is the term used when the pupil "goes shopping" for someone to teach a desired skill.

Excursions

Places of interest visited by a class can become the focus of learning. The mini-excursion is an adaptation for a small group of pupils within a class who are particularly interested in some special area of learning.

People Bank

A book or file of experts in all areas—including the names of individuals, firms, galleries, museums, technicians and their addresses, telephone numbers, hours of availability, and cost—is kept. Names are filed alphabetically and by subject areas.

Mentors

Pupils are matched with an expert in an area in which they are interested. For example, the pupils might wish to meet with a scientist, a lawyer, or an artist. The teacher would then make the initial contact for the pupils and set up "visiting privileges".

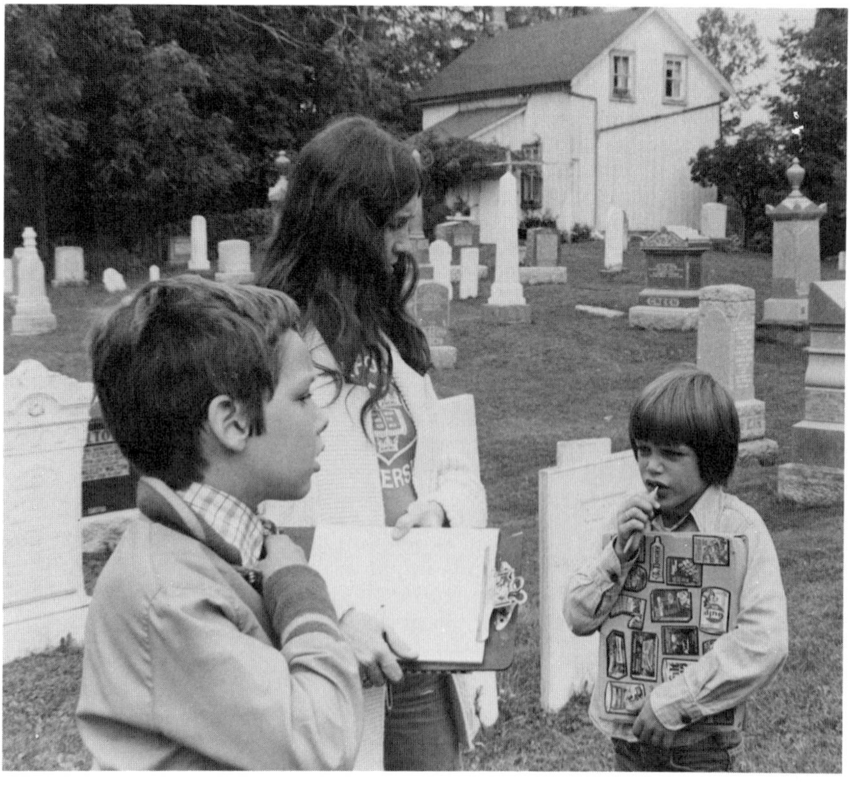

Part II: The Triple Survey

Survey of Departments/Ministries of Education

Provincial regulations and policies affecting gifted and talented students vary widely across Canada, but results of the CEA survey conducted in the fall and winter of 1978-79 indicated that not one department/ministry of education had grants specifically earmarked for the education of these students.

In other ways, however, our departments/ministries provide encouragement for local programs. In Ontario, the gifted student falls under the umbrella of special education. Saskatchewan has furnished short term funding through an "innovative projects program". Prince Edward Island tries to provide supplementary material that teachers are encouraged to use. Every province has its own approach.

This encouragement shows that departments/ministries of education are making an effort to respond to the renewed interest in meeting the needs of gifted and talented students.

Responses to the CEA survey are printed as they were returned, apart from minor editing and condensation.

POLICY

The legal responsibility and authority for education resides with the legislatures of the various provinces. Traditionally, provincial legislatures have delegated their authority to two other agencies. One of these is a central authority, a department or ministry of education, and the other is a local authority or school board. (In Newfoundland the churches have also been very much involved.)

Q. 1 What is the policy of your Department/Ministry regarding the education of gifted and talented students in your province?

BRITISH COLUMBIA The Ministry of Education generally supports programs for gifted and talented students developed by school districts. The former Minister took a personal interest in programs for the gifted and directed that curricula be provided, initially for grades 4, 5 and 12, by September 1979. A contract team at the University of British Columbia, assisted by an Advisory Committee, worked on the curricula.

ALBERTA   Education of the gifted and talented is carried on as one of the responsibilities of school boards. Intellectually gifted pupils are usually accommodated within the regular program, but their work is enriched by more in-depth study of a topic or by special assignments. The artistically gifted person or physically gifted can pursue excellence through the broad curricular offerings. The elementary program has a good balance between academic subjects and those which are creative and expressive. The junior high school program has an academic core with options. The senior high school program has a wide range of subjects.

SASKATCHEWAN   Policy is presently under review by an internal committee of the Department.

MANITOBA   It is the policy of the Department to allow school divisions to conduct special programs in this area if they so desire. At the time of the CEA survey, one metropolitan division planned to begin a pilot program for gifted children in grades 5, 6 and 7 in January 1979.

ONTARIO   "Teachers are responsible for providing each child with the opportunity to achieve levels of competence commensurate with ability."[24] Gifted and talented children are treated as any other exceptional children. The Ministry of Education recognizes the responsibility of school boards to provide programs and services for gifted and talented pupils in their jurisdictions.

QUÉBEC   It is the responsibility of the school boards to create particular services where they are needed.

NEW BRUNSWICK   The Department has no official policy regarding the education of gifted and talented students; however, some school boards attempt to provide some programming for the gifted and talented within their regular school program.

NOVA SCOTIA   School administrators are asked to make every reasonable effort to ensure that individual students at all levels who display superior academic, musical, artistic, linguistic, physical, or other talents or abilities are given the opportunity to develop these abilities. Special classes are not necessary or in most cases practical, but personalized individual programs are both encouraged and supported. No specific programs or courses are presently defined for these students except at upper levels of senior high school, where courses of special challenge are included in certain subject areas. At lower levels, schools are expected to design special activities within listed programs or courses, or to request authorization for special courses individually planned according to the particular talents or abilities identified. The students concerned frequently do not need much of the content of most skill-centred and some content-centred programs and courses in which others are involved. It appears that these children may become bored

---

[24]*Gifted/Talented Children,* Curriculum Ideas for Teachers (Toronto: Ontario Ministry of Education, 1978), p. 2.

and disinterested, which can lead to failure to advance and at times even regression in achievement. Teaching guides or editions of many authorized school programs contain sections that give recommended adjustments and enrichment for these students. The listing of multiple resources in many subject areas means schools may also secure some extra materials which are not used generally in the school concerned. The opportunity to use up to 5% of credit allocation for unlisted materials for special needs of small groups of individuals is a further resource to the school administrator.

PRINCE EDWARD ISLAND   The policy of the Department is to provide a broad program that can be supplemented and adjusted by teachers to meet the needs of a heterogeneous student body. Most school boards have adopted a continuous progress and individualized learning philosophy. This philosophy reduces the need for special programs, since the student is allowed to move on to more challenging materials.

NEWFOUNDLAND   There is no written policy regarding the education of gifted and talented students. However, all schools are encouraged to identify the gifted and to provide, through course arrangements, appropriate learning experiences.

LEGISLATION

The literature suggests that considerable time elapses before specific programs become mandatory. Frequently, the procedures evolve in three phases, which could be described as enabling, encouraging, and enforcing. The first phase, in which school boards are provided with enabling legislation, could take place under existing general guidelines or it could involve new legislation. During the second phase, specific incentives are provided for boards that have accepted the responsibility of new programs, in whole or in part. The third phase, which usually follows after a considerable length of time, produces mandatory legislation. Question 2(a) deals with the area of legislation.

Q. 2(a) State the legal provisions for establishing and conducting gifted and talented programs.

BRITISH COLUMBIA   No special legal provisions are necessary. The Public Schools Act is sufficiently comprehensive to embrace any programs for the gifted and talented that school districts may wish to initiate.

ALBERTA   None specifically.

SASKATCHEWAN   Permissive legislation exists under the Education Act, 1978. Copies of the applicable sections are available upon request.

MANITOBA   There are no legal provisions for establishing and conducting programs for the gifted and talented.

ONTARIO   Legislation is permissive; that is, a school board may provide programs for the gifted and talented. (The Education Act, 1974, section 147, subsection (1) 40).

QUÉBEC   Legal provisions are contained in Regulation 7. The relevant sections are section 10 (activities for the students); 11 (continuous progress); 13 (grouping of students first by age and then by other criteria determined by the school); 25 (the possibility of early advancement to the secondary level); 34 (a choice of courses is available at the secondary level); 35 (subject promotion at the secondary level).

NEW BRUNSWICK   None.

NOVA SCOTIA   The local school system identifies the need for specific types of programs, such as programs for gifted children. Some school boards have identified and are currently piloting particular types of delivery services for such children. These boards organize and monitor the programs and request financial assistance from the Department of Education and the local municipal council.

PRINCE EDWARD ISLAND   No legal provisions exist that refer specifically to programs for the gifted and talented.

NEWFOUNDLAND   There are no legal provisions for establishing programs for the gifted and talented.

Teacher training and certification are the responsibility of the central authority in each province. This centralized control is recognized as an important means of maintaining acceptable standards in the schools. Several provinces have indicated in previous reports that they require special certification and/or qualifications for teachers of exceptional children. The following question was designed to ascertain if this stipulation applies in the case of teachers of gifted and talented children.

Q. 2 (b) State the required qualifications for teachers of gifted and talented programs.

BRITISH COLUMBIA   The Ministry does not set down qualifications for teachers of the gifted, other than those required for any teacher. Not qualifications but outstanding personal qualities are looked upon as essential for good teachers of the gifted. As programs for the gifted expand, provisions for teachers of them may become more explicit.

ALBERTA   None specifically.

SASKATCHEWAN   No special qualifications.

MANITOBA   No special requirements.

ONTARIO   Ontario Teacher's Certificate and Ontario Special Education Qualifications.

QUÉBEC   No special qualifications.

NEW BRUNSWICK   None.

NOVA SCOTIA   There are no special qualifications required of teachers of programs for the gifted and talented: they must possess the minimum qualifications for teaching in the province of Nova Scotia. The local school boards accept full responsibility for the selection and hiring of teachers whom they believe to be capable of carrying through programs for the gifted.

PRINCE EDWARD ISLAND   No special requirements.

NEWFOUNDLAND   None.

FUNDING

Research findings suggest that programs for gifted and talented pupils may result in additional costs. These expenditures may be in the areas of increased staff, extra materials, and transportation. It has also been reported in the literature that additional programs of this nature require incentive grants or other stimulative funds to initiate action on the part of school boards. Prior to the drafting of legislation, supplementary funding is often supplied as encouragement for local jurisdictions.

Q. 3 What additional fundings are made available to boards for establishing and conducting gifted and talented programs?

BRITISH COLUMBIA   No special funding has been determined up to this point, although such is being considered. The Ministry contributes financially to the education of all students through its normal funding processes.

ALBERTA   None.

SASKATCHEWAN   No additional funding through foundation (formula) grants. However, six projects related to gifted students have received short term funding through the Innovative Projects Program.

MANITOBA   No additional funds.

ONTARIO   The funding of special education programs is based upon a weighting factor. In the calculation of funding, itinerant, withdrawal, and resource teachers of gifted programs are given the same weight as teachers of other special education programs. Teachers of self-contained programs for gifted students are not considered in the weighting factor formula.

QUÉBEC   No special funding, except for the possibility of a school board's imposing a special tax for expenses that go over the norm accepted within the balanced budget subventioned by the Ministry of Education.

NEW BRUNSWICK   None.

NOVA SCOTIA   No additional funds are provided for the purpose of establishing and conducting such programs within the credit allocation given to boards based on pupil numbers. A particular board may wish to select from the School Book Bureau listings materials which will guarantee enrichment programs for such children.

PRINCE EDWARD ISLAND   No additional funding.

NEWFOUNDLAND   School boards that wish to do so may avail themselves of the policy of "alternative texts", whereby new programs may be introduced with appropriate approval from the provincial Director of Curriculum.

TRANSPORTATION

A variety of programs may be provided for gifted and talented pupils. These include such options as withdrawal programs, segregated classes, or special schools. Some of the options necessitate transportation of pupils beyond the usual requirements. Understandably, the additional transportation would mean added costs to the participating boards. The next question was asked in order to find out whether school boards were helped with those extra costs.

Q. 4   What additional funds are available for special transportation of gifted and talented students to special programs?

BRITISH COLUMBIA   No additional funds are granted for transportation. The usual regulations regarding funding for busing apply to students living in one town of a school district who have to go to another town for the proper program — gifted or otherwise.

ALBERTA   None.

SASKATCHEWAN   None.

MANITOBA   No additional funds.

ONTARIO   If a school board transports gifted students to special programs it receives grant assistance subject to a maximum approved expenditure. In addition, a transportation grant is provided for home to school travel for segregated classes.

QUÉBEC   At the moment, there is an understanding between school boards that allows students to attend school outside their own school district in order to benefit from any program that is not given by their local school board. Students may receive financial help for transportation and housing.

NEW BRUNSWICK   None.

NOVA SCOTIA   There is no transportation funding for the specific use of gifted and talented students. However, many school boards use the transportation system for the purposes of taking their students to community activities and/or facilities and/or special projects. These opportunities are not restricted only to the gifted and talented, but are made available to all school children.

PRINCE EDWARD ISLAND   No additional funding.

NEWFOUNDLAND   None.

TEACHER EDUCATION

In most provinces, teacher education has been delegated by the central authority to faculties of education in universities. (The next chapter deals with the questionnaires sent to universities as part of the survey.) The following question was asked in order to find out if specific direction is given to universities concerning teachers of gifted and talented pupils.

Q. 5(a) Pre-service: What specific preparation do the teachers in training in your province receive in the area of gifted and talented education?

BRITISH COLUMBIA   It is impossible to categorize what kind of specific training teachers receive in the precise area of educating gifted and talented students. To some extent, this would depend on the inclination of the individual professor or lecturer. It might be one area of exceptionality being considered. Conceivably, the gifted may receive more attention as programs for them become more widespread.

ALBERTA   All teachers are introduced to the exceptional child and his/her characteristics in their course in child psychology or child development.

SASKATCHEWAN   None. Recently both universities have offered a class in this area. Enrolment has been very low.

MANITOBA   No special preparation is provided for teachers in training in the area of educating the gifted and talented, but information on this aspect of education is included in all programs in which teachers in training enrol.

ONTARIO   The pre-service curriculum does not contain specific courses dealing with the teaching of gifted and talented students. Teachers in pre-service may receive specialized instruction re gifted education, depending on the instructor.

QUÉBEC   No special pre-service program expected.

NEW BRUNSWICK   University courses dealing with the exceptional child usually devote a small portion of time to the area of the talented and gifted.

NOVA SCOTIA   There is no special delineation for the training of teachers for children who are gifted or slow learning or of average ability. The province does, however, support a program at Acadia University that offers a diploma in special education to participating teachers. The focus of this program tends to be on children who are handicapped rather than on children with superior endowments.

PRINCE EDWARD ISLAND   No program is provided to train teachers specifically for the gifted and talented. However, the general teacher training program has units that deal with teaching both gifted and other exceptional students.

NEWFOUNDLAND   In the special education degree and diploma programs at Memorial University there are courses on educating the gifted.

Teachers require assistance in upgrading their skills and in keeping up to date on research findings. The provision of information on programs for the gifted and talented is an area where in-service education is important. The next question was posed in order to ascertain the role of the central authority in furnishing in-service assistance for teachers of gifted and talented pupils.

Q. 5(b) In-service: Indicate the training made available to teachers of gifted and talented students by your Department/Ministry: special courses, specific conferences and workshops, special documents, other.

BRITISH COLUMBIA   Specific conferences and workshops and special documents are made available by the Ministry.

ALBERTA   Department persons are encouraged to attend conferences and seminars on the gifted.

SASKATCHEWAN   The Co-ordinator of the Committee on Education of the Gifted has given a few talks. To date, most in-service training has been undertaken by local school jurisdictions.

MANITOBA   None.

ONTARIO   Special courses, specific conferences, and special documents are provided. Consultation with the Ministry and its regional education offices is also available.

QUÉBEC   None.

NEW BRUNSWICK   Some school districts organize one or two in-service sessions related to the talented and gifted as part of their professional development programs.

NOVA SCOTIA   Please refer to the answer to question 5(a).

PRINCE EDWARD ISLAND   None.

NEWFOUNDLAND   None.

RESEARCH AND EVALUATION

It is the responsibility of local school boards to conduct research and evaluate their pupils. The findings of such research are of practical value to local jurisdictions. Departments/ministries of education frequently conduct research on a contractual basis to ascertain the extent and/or effectiveness of certain programs. The following question attempted to learn whether ministries of education had funded research on programs for the gifted and talented.

Q. 6(a) List the research projects on the education of gifted and talented students conducted or sponsored by your Department/Ministry.
(b) Outline your evaluation mechanism for gifted and talented programs.

BRITISH COLUMBIA   (a) Most of the research sponsored by the Ministry of Education respecting the gifted has been of an "in-house" nature, with various officials studying programs undertaken outside of the province or in school districts within the province.

(b) Now, at the time of responding to the CEA survey, there is no provincial mechanism for the evaluation of programs for the gifted and talented; this will develop as the provincial program becomes operational in September 1979. School districts have their own evaluatory procedures for their programs. Those authorized to evaluate programs and teachers in British Columbia, including superintendents, directors of instruction, and principals, evaluate programs for the gifted as they would any other program. In this province it has not been the intention to treat the gifted in isolation from the rest of the student population any more than is necessary to recognize their own degree of exceptionality.

ALBERTA   None.

SASKATCHEWAN   None.

MANITOBA   None.

ONTARIO   (a) (i) "An Investigation of Programs and Performance of Gifted Students in Segregated Enrichment Classes and Integrated Regular Stream Classes"; (ii) "An Analysis of Costs and Effectiveness of Enrichment Programs of Students in Grade Seven and Eight in Selected Boards of Education of Ontario Elementary Schools".

(b) Programs for the gifted can be evaluated by a provincial review. To date none has been done.

QUÉBEC   (a) No such projects at the moment.
  (b) No such evaluation at the moment.

NEW BRUNSWICK   None.

NOVA SCOTIA   Again, the Department of Education does not segregate the gifted and talented in any projects listed, but rather incorporates research on them (for example, achievement assessments) with that on every other school-age child.

PRINCE EDWARD ISLAND   None.

NEWFOUNDLAND   None.

CURRICULUM

A variety of approaches to curriculum development exist across Canada, ranging from a moderately centralized system to a decentralized one. Teachers of gifted and talented pupils frequently require supportive material for their programs.

Q. 7 List the documents, guidelines, pamphlets your Department/Ministry has prepared on the education of gifted and talented students.

BRITISH COLUMBIA   No official documents, guidelines, or pamphlets have been developed by the Ministry of Education respecting programs for the gifted, but a number of working papers have circulated within the Ministry. In addition, many school districts have developed their own guidelines, documentation, and curriculum materials.

ALBERTA   None.

SASKATCHEWAN   The printed material that has been prepared is not considered for general distribution, as its focus is upon specific workshop situations. It includes (i) *The Gifted: A Research Perspective;* (ii) *Programming for the Gifted: A Research Perspective;* (iii) *The Gifted: Delivery of Services.*

MANITOBA   No special guidelines or pamphlets.

ONTARIO   *Gifted/Talented Children* (Curriculum Ideas for Teachers series).

QUÉBEC   At the secondary level we have programs in French (mother tongue), English as a second language, mathematics, and science for gifted students. These programs go more deeply into the subjects, and so are more difficult.

NEW BRUNSWICK   None.

NOVA SCOTIA   The edition of *Public School Programs* that covers the current school year.

PRINCE EDWARD ISLAND   Although no specific programs for the gifted student exist in the province, the provincial course of studies indicates supplementary topics and materials which teachers are encouraged to use in teaching more talented students. Certain courses are provided, particularly in science and mathematics, for students who have above-average ability and/or interest in these areas. Students who have completed grade 12 in some courses can "challenge for university credits", and as a result some students may take second level university courses in their freshman year rather than first level courses.

NEWFOUNDLAND   None.

ASSOCIATIONS

The involvement of associations and parent groups occasionally provides a stimulus to central authorities and/or local jurisdictions to provide additional programs or services. The literature suggests that associations with an interest in gifted pupils are increasing across North America.

Q. 8 List the parent and professional associations for gifted and talented children and youth in the province.

BRITISH COLUMBIA   The Ministry understands that teachers of the gifted have recently organized a provincial specialist association under the B.C. Teachers' Federation. Its official title is The Association of Educators of Gifted, Talented and Creative Children in British Columbia. So far as is known, no comparable parents' organization exists.

ALBERTA   An Alberta chapter of the Council for Exceptional Children.

SASKATCHEWAN   Regina Association for the Gifted; a Saskatchewan chapter of the Council for Exceptional Children.

MANITOBA   A Manitoba chapter of the Council for Exceptional Children.

ONTARIO   Association for Bright Children; Scarborough Association for Gifted Education (SAGE); The Association for the Gifted (TAG); an Ontario chapter of the Council for Exceptional Children.

QUÉBEC   The Association for the Gifted in Canada (TAG—Canada).[25]

NEW BRUNSWICK   None.

NOVA SCOTIA   A Nova Scotia chapter of the Council for Exceptional Children; Association for Teachers of Exceptional Children.

PRINCE EDWARD ISLAND   No such associations exist in this province.

NEWFOUNDLAND   None.

---

[25]The Association for the Gifted in Canada is a national association. Information may be obtained from Dr. Bruce M. Shore of the Faculty of Education, McGill University.

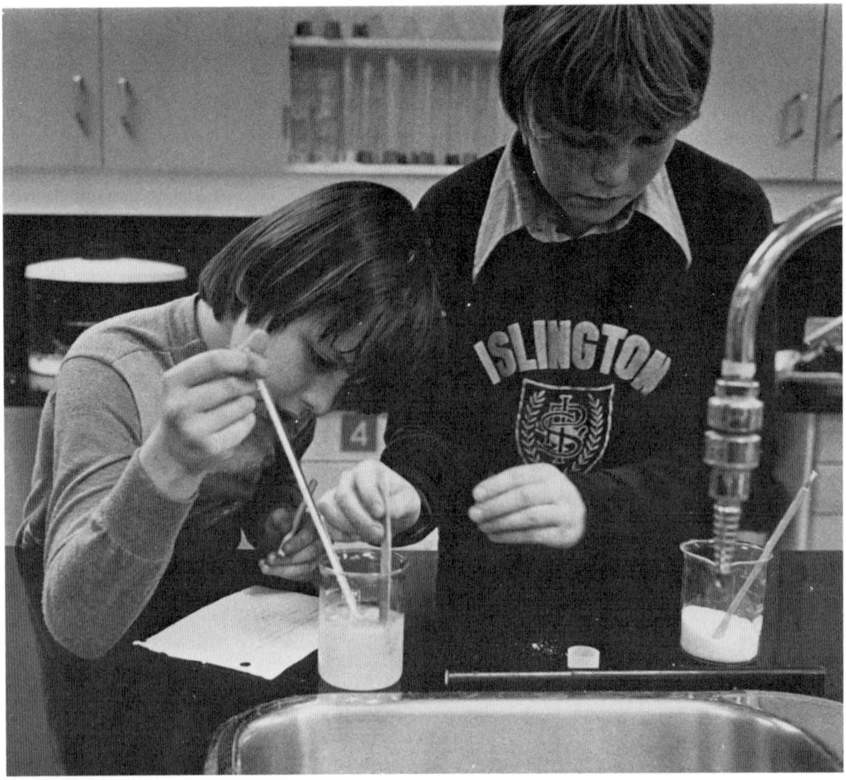
ISLINGTON

Survey of Faculties of Education

There's a strange irony about the status of the gifted student on a Canadian university campus.

On the one hand, no group gets higher praise from a university than those who have a gift for grasping difficult concepts, a genius for seeing a new perspective, a limitless academic curiosity, and who usually win the prestigious awards and scholarships.

Yet few faculties of education of Canadian universities are doing much to promote improved understanding of the gifted student's needs in the grades that lead to higher education.

How that gifted or talented student is educated before university does not appear to be a concern with much priority in the overwhelming majority of faculties of education, judging from the CEA survey, in which 21 completed questionnaires were received in the late fall and early winter of 1978-79 (an excellent return that included both larger and smaller institutions and represented all 10 provinces).

The questionnaire sought information on how education for the gifted and talented student is reflected in teacher preparation, including pre-service training, graduate studies, and professional development activities.

The fact that some faculties of education have programs focused on preparing teachers for gifted and talented students is encouraging. The CEA survey also found some excellent professional development programs for teachers in this area. But the general picture that emerges from the survey is that

- Universities tend to incorporate preparation for teaching the gifted or talented into the broad field of special education.
- Programs that focus on the needs of gifted and talented students are not common in Canadian faculties of education.
- Very few faculties of education offer graduate courses in this area.

Here are the specific results of the survey.

TEACHER PREPARATION PROGRAMS

Q. 1 Does your university offer programs in preparing teachers for gifted and talented students?

There were 21 responses to this question. Five universities reported that they had such programs in operation. Sixteen responded that they had no programs; however, several of these qualified their reply by saying that while they had no specific preparation program for teaching the gifted, this preparation was integrated into the basic program.

Q. 2 Does your teacher education program offer: full credit courses dealing with the education of gifted and talented students? Courses that contain lectures on the education of gifted and talented students? Specify.

There were basically two types of teacher preparation offered: (a) specific courses on the education of the gifted and talented were offered in nine of the 21 universities that replied to this question; (b) portions of courses or sessions on the education of the gifted and talented were offered by 17 universities, including the nine that offered complete courses in that area.

Four universities reported no involvement in preparing teachers for the gifted. The degree of involvement of the other 17 respondents varied from "a section of work" or "a short module" on the gifted in a general course, to "a selection of two credit courses (1 ½ units each)" or "one full class in the area of gifted and talented students".

GRADUATE PROGRAMS

Q. 3 Does your university have a graduate program?
Q. 4 Does your university have a graduate program in special education? If yes, does it include material on gifted and talented students?
Q. 5 Does the graduate program offer courses on the education of gifted and talented students? Specify.

Seventeen universities reported that they offered graduate programs. Of these, 10 indicated that they had a graduate program in special education. At five universities material on giftedness was regularly included in the graduate special education program, and at a sixth arrangements could be made to do so. Information was not obtained on the remaining four universities.

However, when universities were asked to respond about a graduate program on the education of gifted and talented students, only four reported they had such program options. Two of the 17 that answered in the negative stated that reading courses were available in that area.

PROFESSIONAL DEVELOPMENT ACTIVITIES

Q. 6 Does your university provide seminars, workshops, or other professional development activities for teachers of the gifted and talented programs? Specify.

Replies to this question indicated a wide variety in the degree of involvement of faculties of education in this area of teacher education.

Some universities were extremely active in providing professional development programs for teachers. Two good examples were the University of Saskatchewan's program for pre-school gifted and talented children and the project headed by Dr. Stanley Blank of the University of British Columbia for gifted students of several school districts of the province. On the other hand, a number of institutions (11) reported no involvement at all in this type of professional activity for teachers.

GENERAL OBSERVATIONS

The information provided by the survey of faculties of education would seem to indicate that, generally, preparing teachers to educate gifted and talented students is not a priority. The scarcity of specific programs in this area and the lack of involvement of many universities in relevant professional development activities support this observation. The following table summarizes the participation of the responding universities. (For a complete breakdown of the response from the universities, please see Appendix B.)

TYPE OF INVOLVEMENT	YES	NO	NA*	TOTAL
Programs in preparing teachers for gifted/talented students	5	16		21
Courses	9	12		21
Lectures	17	3	1	21
Graduate programs in special education containing material on gifted/talented students	6	10	5	21
Graduate programs offering courses on the education of gifted/talented students	4	17**		21
Professional development activities	10	11		21

* No answer.
**Two of the 17 stated that reading courses were available.

Clearly, the results of the survey establish the presence of "gifted education" within the framework of the universities. Some universities reported specific projects in this area; others were planning new activities. The findings lead the authors to conclude that there is a need for a systematic approach by faculties of education to providing teachers for the education of gifted and talented students. Those few universities that are involved in this area would certainly provide a sound foundation for future development.

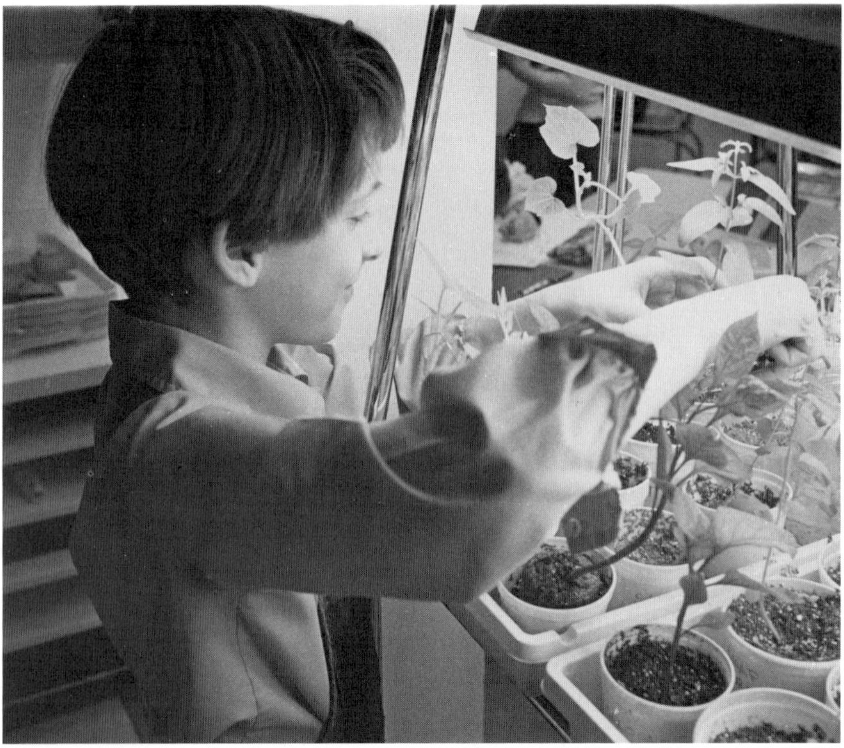

Survey of School Boards

The summarized results of the 20 questions asked in the CEA survey provide possibly the clearest picture yet available of how local school boards in Canada are identifying their gifted and talented students, and of how they are providing for the students' special needs.

In the fall of 1978, 586 operating school boards, or the majority of boards in each province, were sent questionnaires. Included in the 586 were all the largest school systems and a great number of the smaller ones; it has been estimated that they administered the education of about 97% of the pupils in public schools and publicly supported separate schools in the ten provinces. As well, a questionnaire was sent to the Yukon Territory and another to the Northwest Territory. The replies received numbered 316 (54%), an above-average response for a mailed survey. The authors feel that the returns from school boards are representative of the provinces: respondents included large and small boards in both urban and rural areas.

Two of the interesting pieces of information received in the survey were that class sizes for gifted and talented students ranged from 4 to 40, and that the classroom teacher carried a great deal of the responsibility for specially adapting programs. We found that teachers were using a wide spectrum of resources to encourage learning. Some of the more unusual community resources named were pioneer villages, oil wells, ranches, Indian reserves, and mines.

Among the difficulties encountered by school boards in attempting to provide for gifted and talented students were those of finding funds for special programs and of defending their costs to the local community. Many boards reported, too, that their teachers found it difficult to locate the courses they needed to better equip themselves for educating the gifted and talented.

The parent who reads the following section should have a clear idea of the school board's role in providing education. The legal responsibility and authority for education in Canada rests with the provincial governments. They, in turn, delegate varying amounts of responsibility and authority to local school boards. Each province has established, through its acts and regulations and administrative instructions, certain minimum standards which must be met.

Beyond these minimum standards, the local school board is allowed to make provision for its own priorities, based upon the particular needs of its community. The board's challenge is to meet the needs of the community as well as imagination and finances will permit.

In terms of education for gifted and talented students, the local school board is the most visible target for parents who urge expanded courses and *opportunities. Yet the CEA survey of provincial departments/ministries of education found that no provincial authority in Canada provided funding to school boards specifically for gifted education programs, though some provided incentives to encourage the specialized programs and services.*

RESULTS OF THE SURVEY

The number of questionnaires returned by the various provinces and territories is shown below.

British Columbia	41	New Brunswick	14
Alberta	43	Nova Scotia	15
Saskatchewan	33	Prince Edward Island	3
Manitoba	29	Newfoundland	12
Ontario	64	Yukon Territory	1
Québec	54	Northwest Territory	1
		Unidentified	6

An analysis of the responses, question by question, now follows.

Q. 1 Does your board make special provisions for gifted and talented students?

Percentage of total respondents who indicated Yes: 37

Provincial breakdown of affirmative replies by percentages:

British Columbia	43	Québec	16
Alberta	31	New Brunswick	30
Saskatchewan	35	Nova Scotia	38
Manitoba	35	Prince Edward Island	33
Ontario	61	Newfoundland	23

(Note: The replies from the Yukon and the Northwest Territory, as well as the replies on the six questionnaires that were returned without identification, were negative.)

The initial question was designed to find out if school boards were providing for the needs of gifted and talented students. The table which presents the results suggests that only a small portion of gifted students are receiving special programs and services. This may not be entirely the situation. Many school boards stated that individual schools and/or individual teachers were responsible for providing for the needs of gifted and talented students. Similarly to the provincial authority, which delegates responsibility to the local school boards, these boards have delegated the responsibility to schools or teachers. It is not possible from this survey to determine if individual schools or teachers have accepted the mandate.

Many of the respondents that answered question 1 in the negative indicated that a special committee of the board had been formed to report on the need for programs for the gifted. These statements support the research literature, which shows renewed interest in gifted and talented students. In addition, a significant number of respondents stated that a specific person within the central office staff had been designated as responsible for programs and services for the gifted and talented. A number of boards had given this person the status of consultant or coordinator of gifted programs. Approximately one third of those reporting across Canada indicated that pilot projects were being conducted by their boards or were being planned for 1979. Therefore, the reader is again cautioned that the results shown for question 1 may present only part of the picture.

Q. 2 Types of programs offered.

The literature suggests a variety of programs and services that could be provided for gifted and talented students. In the questionnaire, we listed the most important of these. The figures below indicate the number of respondents who conducted the various programs.

Special schools for the gifted and talented		6
Full-time classes for the gifted and talented		21
Part-time classes for the gifted and talented		48
Special creativity or resource centre		43
serving one school	13	
serving a family of schools	10	
serving all schools within the board	20	
Saturday morning program		12
After school program		8
Summer program		13
Tutorial assistance		27
Independent study		63
Special subjects		35

Because several boards were operating a variety of programs, a total for these responses is not meaningful.

Respondents indicated that a number of modifications had been made to the programs listed. These included the following: teachers receiving enrichment materials through the media centre, grouping of gifted students within the regular class, a pull-out program for a short period of time per week, an itinerant teacher available in all schools to assist individual teachers with gifted student programs.

The figures summarizing responses to question 2 do not include the planned projects that became operational in 1979 after the survey was made.

Q. 3 Does your board accelerate gifted and talented students?

Responses to question 2 suggested that a variety of programs and services were being provided for gifted students. A majority of the boards emphasized that their programs consisted of enrichment activities for pupils; nevertheless, this section of the survey attempted to find out how prevalent acceleration programs were in the education of gifted children.

	No. of respondents stating	
	Yes	No
Does your board accelerate gifted/talented students?	55	63
Do students skip grades?	27	25

The literature suggests that there is a difference of opinion on the question of acceleration, and the results of our survey reinforce this impression. The number of boards advocating acceleration was almost equal to those who provided enrichment activities and no acceleration. Many of the boards that supported acceleration described a continuous progress plan which allowed pupils to complete their elementary school program in one year less than the normal period. It appeared from the returns that a number of jurisdictions allowed individual pupils to skip grades. The comment accompanying some of the questionnaires indicated that this took place in years 3 or 4 or 5. Respondents frequently wrote that acceleration was used only when it was in the best interests of the child and did not interfere with his/her physical, social, and emotional welfare. When we consider the numerical response together with the comments, it appears that the respondents saw acceleration as a possible alternative which should be decided on an individual basis.

Q. 4(a) Does your board have a specific policy for educating gifted and talented students?

Respondents stating yes: 26.1%   Respondents stating no: 73.9%

As shown, most boards did not have a stated policy for the education of gifted students at the time of our survey. A number of boards replied that their general policy was sufficient to ensure individual programs for gifted pupils. In addition, a significant number of respondents indicated that a policy statement was being prepared and would be available by the fall of 1979. The above results indicate that approximately one quarter of responding school boards had a specific policy dealing with this aspect of exceptionality. These figures should not be interpreted as representing the percentage of boards providing programs.

Q. 4(b) Does your program for gifted and talented students come under the jurisdiction of:

	Yes responses
Special Education Department	62.8%
Curriculum Department	31.4%
Other	5.8%

There appear to be jurisdictional problems here. In some provinces the administration of programs for gifted and talented students has been assigned specifically to the special education section. In those provinces, there was little hesitation on the part of school boards in answering this question. In provinces without specific legislation or policy, boards had apparently assigned the gifted programs to individuals. If the individual was working in the special education section, then the program was placed under the jurisdiction of that department, but a variety of alternative administrative patterns was indicated by the responses categorized as "other". These included assigning the administration of gifted pupils' programs to such sections as student services, program department, or support services. A number of boards replied that their programs were under the jurisdiction of both the special education department and the curriculum department. We cannot comment on the implications of these situations without studying the organizational charts.

Q. 5 Rate in order of importance (from 1-7 with 1 being most important) the method used by your board to identify gifted and talented students.

The ranking in the table below represents the collective responses to this question. Only those boards which conducted programs for selected students were counted in the analysis.

Teacher selection	1
Individual test—psychological	2
Individual test—academic	3
Group test—academic	4
Group test—psychological	5
Parent selection	6
Peer selection	7

Most of the boards indicated that sophisticated procedures of screening and identification took place. Several boards signified that they would use the first five indicators listed above as screening devices. It was apparent from the results that the teacher played a key role in the identification of gifted students. The returns also showed the reluctance of some boards to use group psychological tests in their schools.

In almost all instances, parent selection and peer selection were not regarded as important. A few respondents indicated that they were encouraged by parents to provide special programs for gifted pupils.

Results from this question suggest a problem in defining the terms gifted and talented. Recent reports imply that this problem exists in other countries as well. Several researchers have proposed multi-dimensional definitions which make it very difficult to identify students who could be classified as gifted.

Q. 6 Indicate who is responsible for the admission of gifted and talented students to special programs.

	Percentage of total respondents
An admission committee at the board level	9%
An admission committee at the school level	22%
A school superintendent	14%
A special coordinator	17%
A school principal	38%

Understandably, the results obtained from this section of the survey reflect the specific programs selected in responding to question 2. What is also apparent is the key role played by the principal in a large group of school boards. In addition to the boards which indicated that the principal had the total responsibility for admitting gifted and talented students to special programs, a number of other boards reported that the principal chaired the selection committee. Boards which are contemplating the establishment of programs for the gifted will note the variety of approaches in operation.

Q. 7 Indicate the criteria required before a student is admitted to a program for the gifted and talented.

In most instances, a combination of criteria were utilized; therefore, the response percentages shown below total more than 100.

	Percentage of total respondents
Group I.Q. test result	31%
Individual I.Q. test result	40%
Aptitude test result	27%
Parent permission	69%
High performance	92%
A specific minimum I.Q.	35%

It appears that high performance is a criterion used by most boards. Several respondents suggested that high performance could be measured in a number of ways. This implies that giftedness is a multi-faceted phenomenon, a point supported by recent literature on the gifted.

Elsewhere in the literature it has been reported that there is a reluctance to utilize intelligence test results in admission procedures, but this fact is not entirely substantiated by the replies to our survey. Approximately one third of the respondents to this question indicated that a minimum I.Q. was required before a student was admitted to the program for the gifted. The minimum acceptable I.Q. ranged from 115 to 145, with the average being 130. Several respondents emphasized that the I.Q. was used with discretion and in conjunction with other indicators. (Note: boards were not asked to give the names of the intelligence tests that they used; thus in considering this data one should be aware of the norm differences among tests.)

Q. 8 Indicate the grade levels at which your programs for gifted and talented students begin and terminate.

	Elementary		Secondary	
Beginning grade	K	11%	7	10%
	1	10%	8	15%
	2	9%	9	18%
	3	8%	10	25%
	4	17%	11	5%
	5	11%	not specified	27%
	6	6%		
	7	3%		
	not specified	25%		
Terminating grade	6	25%	9	5%
	7	25%	10	10%
	8	25%	11	0%
	not specified	25%	12	50%
			13	20%
			not specified	15%

The results of asking this question were difficult to interpret, due to the varying organizational patterns in operation across Canada. For example, the traditional K-8 and 9-13 pattern in Ontario produced one set of results and the K-6 and 7-12 organizational pattern in some other provinces produced another. We appreciated the accompanying comments which clarified the returns.

It appears that a pattern for beginning programs for the gifted has not been established across Canada. The data suggest that once a program is started it usually continues until the pupil changes schools. If a program is conducted in a K-6 school chances are that it will terminate at grade 6; similarly, a program in a K-8 school is likely to end at grade 8. In the secondary panel a similar pattern emerges. This partially explains the high percentage of programs which terminate at the grade 12 level. The researchers suggest that the large number of unspecified responses was due to the unique organizational patterns in some school jurisdictions.

Q. 9 Indicate the special transportation provisions made for gifted and talented students.

	Percentage of total respondents with gifted programs
To special schools for gifted and talented	5%
To resource centres	9%
For field trips	36%

Data secured by asking this question suggest that most boards do not provide additional transportation for pupils attending gifted and talented programs. As revealed earlier in this report, one of the findings of our survey of departments/ministries of education was that there was little supplementary funding available from them for this purpose. Therefore, most boards answering question 9 stated that parents were responsible for providing transportation to special programs for gifted students. A number of urban boards replied that public transportation was used and that pupils in special programs were issued bus tickets. This figure is included in the 5% indicated above.

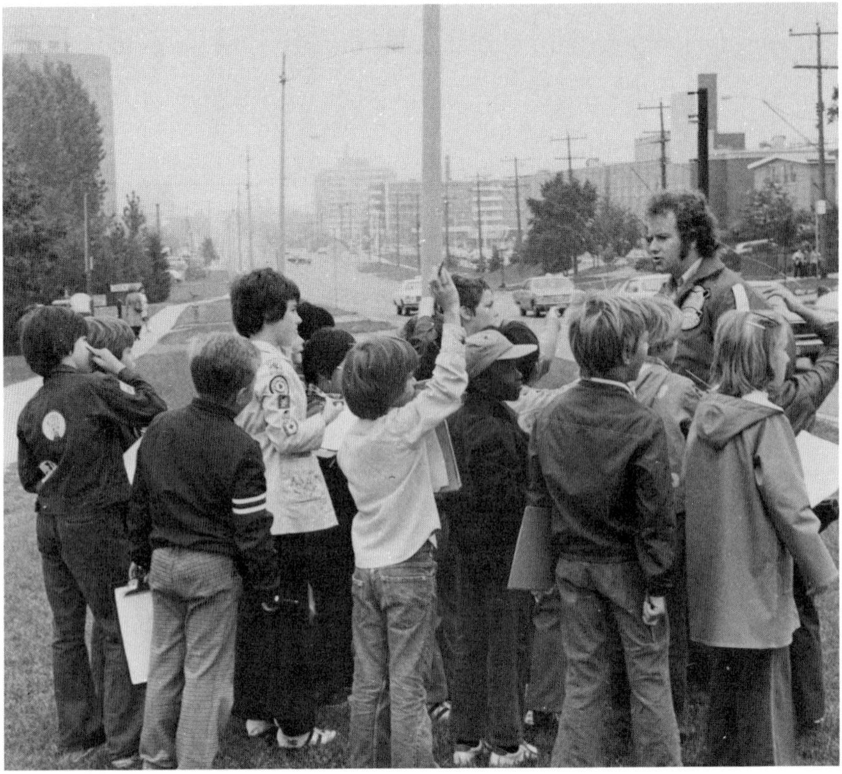

The literature suggests that it is essential for programs for gifted children to contain a variety of experiences. The results of our survey show support for this view: a significant number of boards were providing additional funding for field trips and excursions.

Several of the respondents indicated that they have had excellent cooperation from parents in providing transportation. Understandably, most of these comments came from urban centres; the problem of transportation is more acute in rural jurisdictions.

Q. 10 Does your board have special curriculum materials for gifted and talented programs?

Respondents stating yes: 69%   Respondents stating no: 31%

    Specifically
      program outline   25%
      teaching materials   67%
      special equipment   15%
    (Note: Percentages add up to more than 100
    since categories are not mutually exclusive.)

Our data indicate that many school boards develop curricula at the system level and distribute the material to the schools. Other jurisdictions rely on curriculum specialists in the schools to supplement provincial guidelines. A number of respondents wrote that the adjustments necessary in curriculum for gifted pupils must be made by classroom teachers; others that groups of teachers worked cooperatively in each school to adapt the curriculum to individual pupil needs.

Fifteen per cent of the respondents indicated that special equipment was provided. This varied from special library facilities to audio-visual equipment to special furniture. In several school systems, additional equipment had been purchased by Home and School or other parent associations.

Q. 11 Indicate the personnel responsible for your gifted and talented program.

The positive responses of boards that had said they made special provisions for gifted and talented students (question 1) were calculated by percentages as follows:

    Coordinator of gifted and talented students   11%
    Consultant of gifted and talented students   12%
    Resource teacher   42%
    Itinerant teachers   8%
    Classroom teachers   19%
    Other (includes superintendent of special   8%
      education, area superintendent, principal,
      special education coordinator, etc.)

Special incentives in funding may have enabled some jurisdictions to appoint personnel to direct programs for the gifted and talented. Our data imply that the resource teacher is a key figure in the administration of such programs.

Nineteen per cent of the respondents indicated that classroom teachers were responsible for the gifted programs. This figure just applied to the boards which replied in the affirmative to question 1 of the survey. An additional group of respondents indicated that teachers were responsible for adapting their programs to fit the needs of individual students. The literature suggests that this may not happen unless the teacher is given assistance. Our results support such conjecture, as a total of 50% of those whose replies to question 11 are given here indicated the use of resource or itinerant teachers to facilitate the program.

Q. 12 Indicate the types of in-service training that your board provides for teachers of gifted and talented students.

	Percentage of total respondents
Special courses	10%
Special workshops	47%
Special provisions to attend courses and workshops outside your board jurisdiction	65%
An orientation session prior to assigning teachers to gifted and talented programs	18%

The responses total more than 100%, since many boards were providing a combination of in-service experiences. A strong plea for assistance in this area was made by numerous respondents. Requests were being submitted to faculties of education to provide courses for teachers of gifted students. Several of the respondents indicated that teachers frequently had to travel considerable distances to locate such courses.

Approximately 10% of the respondents indicated that their boards did not provide any form of in-service training for teachers of gifted and talented students. Several of these wrote that personnel were not available with expertise in the area of giftedness.

It appears from our data that an interest in courses for teachers of gifted and talented students is prevalent across Canada. The chapter in this report dealing with services provided by universities furnishes additional information on this subject.

Q. 13 Indicate the resources used in developing and implementing your gifted and talented programs.

	Percentage of boards with programs that used the resource
A. Resources within the school	
special provision within the school library	67%
special provision within the school music program	32%
special provision within the school art program	30%
special provision within the school gym	22%

B. *Community resources*

community college and university personnel and facilities	36%
service clubs and agencies	22%
libraries	59%
museums	56%
industry	25%
senior citizens	22%
professionals	47%
tradesmen	22%
community workers	28%
historical buildings and other community facilities	47%

Responses to the first part of the question indicated that boards were using a multi-dimensional approach to giftedness. Pupils who demonstrated outstanding talents in art, music, or physical education were being provided with programs.

Understandably, there was considerable overlap in the responses to this question. A number of respondents signified that they used combinations of available resources. The comparatively high response to the use of museums suggests that many of the programs were being conducted in urban areas where such facilities were available.

Additional community resources were listed by many of the respondents. These included ranches, oil wells, mines, Indian reserves, and pioneer villages.

The results gained from asking this question may not accurately represent some of the programs being conducted at the secondary level. Such courses frequently are given within the regular school, using available staff members and special equipment such as laboratories or computers.

Q. 14 Indicate the total number of gifted and talented students in:

Special schools	1,318
Special full-time classes	4,324
Special part-time classes	3,361
Saturday morning programs	1,770
After school programs	484
Summer programs	943
Independent study	1,327
Total	13,527

The figures represent the total numbers reported by the boards that indicated they made special provisions for gifted and talented students. Several boards did not reply to this question. They furnished comments to the effect that they did not identify gifted pupils as such, but had individual teachers respond to individual pupil needs.

There may be some overlap in the above figures. A few boards indicated that some pupils may take advantage of more than one program, for example a special part-time program and a Saturday morning program.

(Note: Many gifted and talented students are in private schools. Such schools were not included in the survey.)

Q. 15 Indicate the total actual number of gifted and talented students in your programs for gifted and talented students.

Total response: 12,717 students

The discrepancy between the numbers presented in the replies to questions 14 and 15 appears to refer to the description of programs and services. Several respondents indicated that the number of students on an independent study program was difficult to quantify. In addition, a few school boards did not reply to question 15 with an actual number, but simply stated that approximately 2-5% of their student population was being provided with services. When interpreting these figures, one must remember that out of a survey of 588 school systems, replies were received from 316. We assume that most of the 272 surveyed boards that did not respond did not have special programs for gifted and talented students.

Q. 16 Indicate the average enrolment for each full-time gifted and talented class.

Number of pupils	Percentage of boards responding
1-5	3%
6-10	15%
11-15	12%
16-20	18%
21-25	28%
26-30	18%
over 30	6%

Responses to this question indicated that the size of classes for gifted pupils ranged from a low of 4 to a high of 40. The most repeated numbers were in the 21-25 range. The replies to question 2 showed that a comparatively small number of boards conducted special schools or special classes for gifted students. It appears from the data presented here that most of the classes were considered as part of the regular school and contained a similar number of students.

In the survey of provincial authorities, none of the departments/ministries of education indicated that they were providing special funding for gifted classes; therefore, local school boards would have to furnish additional funds for this purpose. When class sizes are part of the negotiation process, a reduction for any type of special program is difficult to justify.

Q. 17 Indicate the average number of gifted and talented students for whom each resource teacher would be responsible.

In answering an earlier question, a significant number of boards indicated that programs for gifted and talented students were conducted by resource teachers. The table below shows the number of pupils for whom each resource teacher was responsible. The data do not reveal if the resource teachers were also responsible for other aspects of special education.

Number of pupils	Percentage of boards using one resource teacher for that number of pupils
1-5	14%
6-10	11%
11-15	25%
16-20	14%
21-25	11%
26 or over	25%

The 14% figure for resource teachers working with 1-5 pupils may be deceiving. In some cases the respondents indicated that classroom teachers acted as resource teachers for individual pupils in their classrooms. It is difficult to understand how such a person would have the time to provide a comprehensive program for a group of gifted pupils.

Q. 18 Indicate the approximate additional cost incurred by your board for the following services:

	Percentage of total respondents with gifted programs	Range
Consultative services for gifted/talented students	15%	$ 500 to $ 50,000
Coordinator for gifted/talented students	8%	$ 500 to $ 33,000
Teachers for gifted/talented students	23%	$1,000 to $150,000
Transportation for gifted/talented students	12%	$ 400 to $ 76,000
Equipment for gifted/talented students	20%	$ 200 to $ 10,000
Material for gifted/talented students	30%	$ 200 to $ 48,000

The variability in funding procedures throughout Canada made the responses to this question difficult to interpret. Therefore, we will provide a brief description of each of its sections.

Most boards indicated that their programs for gifted and talented students cost additional money. Approximately one third of the respondents who were conducting special programs for the gifted placed a monetary figure on the actual cost. A number of others reported that it would be impossible to present figures. Several suggested that no grants

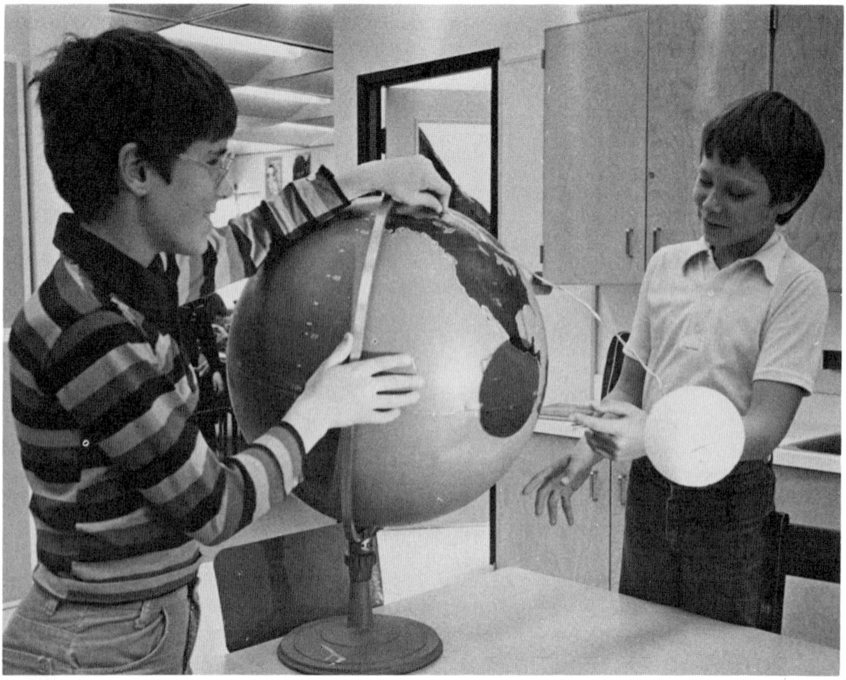

were receivable from the provincial government, therefore it was not necessary to cost out additional funds required to conduct the program.

Fifteen per cent of the boards responding that they conducted special programs for the gifted stated that additional funds were allocated for consultative services. The range varied from a small percentage of one person's time to the availability of two full-time consultants. Several respondents indicated that a special education consultant looked after programs for the gifted along with other duties and a breakdown of costs had not been made.

A similar situation existed in regard to the position of coordinator. Eight per cent of the respondents indicated a cost figure. The range of reported figures shows a wide variation in costs. One board wrote that the equivalent of 1.5 persons were designated as coordinators of gifted programs.

An incurred cost for teachers was given by 23% of the responding boards. The range suggests flexibility in allocating staff. For example, several teachers reported on spent one half-day per week on programs for the gifted, others worked on these programs full time. Many respondents suggested that a cost figure in this area was impossible to arrive at, since the teachers had to be hired anyway. Such teachers were paid the same as those teaching a regular class. The lack of provincial funding for gifted programs contributed to the variability of responses in this section. Several boards stated that the Saturday morning programs were funded by special grants.

Twelve per cent of those reporting gifted programs identified a cost for transportation of pupils. An earlier question discovered that only a small percentage of boards provided transportation of pupils to gifted programs. Our data suggest that most of the additional costs in this area are being absorbed by the boards. At a time of diminishing resources it may be difficult for boards to sustain such expenditures.

One fifth of the boards estimated additional costs for equipment. This item was difficult to separate from the item on materials. Many boards combine their budget allocations for equipment and supplies. It appears that major expenses are not a factor in this area. Programs for the gifted and talented are more expensive in terms of personnel. This applies to all areas of exceptionality.

As mentioned previously, school boards frequently are required to justify additional costs. One respondent suggested that to conduct a successful program for the gifted would cost considerable money, and at the present time his school board was not prepared to provide the necessary funding.

Q. 19 How does your board evaluate your gifted and talented programs?

	Percentage of total respondents with gifted programs
Achievement testing	35%
Program review	70%
No evaluation reported	20%

The percentages add up to more than 100 because several boards replied that a variety of evaluation techniques were used, including both achievement testing and program review. One fifth of the respondents indicated that no evaluation of the program took place. Many of these boards wrote that an evaluation procedure was in preparation, a few stating that the additional costs of the programs provided the necessity for evaluation. One board described a comprehensive evaluation schedule involving students, parents, teachers, principals, and coordinators, and using a variety of data-gathering techniques.

Answers to question 11 showed that a number of boards left it to the individual teacher to meet the needs of gifted and talented pupils. In responding to question 19, these boards indicated that the teachers evaluated the program.

Q. 20 Indicate the criteria in order of importance (from 1 to 7 with 1 being the most important) for the selection of teachers for gifted and talented programs.

Ninety-five per cent of the boards stating that they had a program for the gifted and talented replied to this question. The ranking in the table below represents the collective response.

Flexibility	1
Commitment	2
Creativity	3
Intellectual ability	4
Human relations	5
Personality	6
Academic qualifications	7

The results presented above are not meaningful in light of the variety of responses. We recognize the problem in defining and measuring the traits listed. We are also aware that the reporting of averages tells very little about the responses. A visual examination of the entire data indicates no pattern of answers. Many of the respondents indicated that all of these traits were important and they were ranking them with great reservation. It was apparent that many boards wanted personnel with a combination of the listed qualities. We must also remember that the questionnaire was usually completed by one person. That person may have ranked the items arbitrarily. We would hesitate to base predictions on the responses to this question.

Appendixes

Appendix A: Works Cited

Dow, Ian, and Bert Donnelly. "Differentiated Programs for Gifted Intermediate Students". University of Ottawa/Ontario Ministry of Education, 1977. Unpublished report.

Garrison, K.C., and D.G. Force. *The Psychology of Exceptional Children,* 4th ed. New York: Ronald Press, 1965.

Gifted/Talented Children. Curriculum Ideas for Teachers series. Toronto: Ontario Ministry of Education, 1978.

Hollingworth, Leta S. *Gifted Children: Their Nature and Nurture.* New York: Macmillan Co., 1926.

Horwitz, E.L. "Gifted Children". *Children Today,* Vol. 2, No. 1 (January-February 1973), pp. 27-30.

Lamson, Edna E.A. *A Study of Young Gifted Children in Senior High School.* Contributions to Education No. 424. New York: Bureau of Publications, Teachers College, Columbia University, 1930.

Mirman, Norman. "Education of the Gifted in the 70s". *The Gifted Child Quarterly,* Vol. 15, No. 3 (Autumn 1971), pp. 217-224.

Project Equity. Ottawa: Carleton Board of Education, 1973.

Samuda, Ronald J. *Psychological Testing of American Minorities: Issues and Consequences.* New York: Dodd Mead & Co., 1975.

Sumption, M.R., and E.M. Luecking. *Education of the Gifted.* New York: Ronald Press, 1960.

Terman, L.M., and M.H. Oden. *The Gifted Child Grows Up: Twenty-five Year Follow-up of a Superior Group.* Genetic Studies of Genius, Vol. IV. Stanford, Calif.: Stanford University Press, 1947.

U.S. Office of Education. *Education of the Gifted and Talented.* Vol. 1, *Report to the Congress of the United States by the U.S. Commissioner of Education;* Vol. 2, *Background Papers.* Washington, D.C.: Washington Monitoring Service by the Editors of *Education U.S.A.,* 1971.

Whitmore, J. *The Gifted Underachiever.* Nashville, Tenn.: Geo. Peabody College for Teachers.

Wolfle, Dael. "Diversity of Talent". In J.L. French (ed.), *Educating the Gifted,* rev. ed., pp. 23-35. New York: Holt, Rinehart & Winston Inc., 1964.

Appendix B: Individual Responses from Universities

QUESTION AREA				RESPONDING UNIVERSITIES				
Does your university offer:	Alberta	British Columbia	Calgary	Concordia	Laval	Manitoba	McGill
A. Programs in preparing teachers for gifted/talented students?							
Full credit courses?	NO	YES	YES	NO	NO	NO	NO
Lectures?	NO	YES	YES	YES	NO	NO	YES
	YES	YES	YES	YES	YES	YES	YES
B. A graduate program in special education that includes material on gifted/talented students?	YES	YES	YES	NO	INO*	YES	YES**
A graduate program that offers courses on the education of gifted/talented students?	YES	YES	NO	NO***	NO	YES	NO***
C. Professional development activities for teachers of the gifted/talented?	YES	YES	NO	NO	NO	NO	YES

*Information not obtained
**Special arrangements can be made to include such material
***Reading courses may be arranged

QUESTION AREA

RESPONDING UNIVERSITIES

Does your university offer:	Memorial	Moncton	Montréal	Ottawa	Prince Edward Island	Québec (at Montréal)	Québec (at Rimouski)
A. Programs in preparing teachers for gifted/talented students?							
Full credit courses?	NO	NO	NO	NO	NO	NO	NO
Lectures?	YES	YES	NO	YES	NO	NO	NO
	YES	YES	INO*	YES	YES	NO	NO
B. A graduate program in special education that includes material on gifted/talented students?	NO	INO	INO	NO	NO	INO	NO
A graduate program that offers courses on the education of gifted/talented students?	NO	NO	NO	NO	NO	NO	NO
C. Professional development activities for teachers of the gifted/talented?	NO	YES	NO	YES	NO	NO	NO

*Information not obtained

QUESTION AREA

RESPONDING UNIVERSITIES

Does your university offer:	Queen's	Regina	Sainte-Anne	Saskatchewan	Toronto	Victoria	York
A. Programs in preparing teachers for gifted/talented students?	NO	NO	NO	YES	YES	NO	YES
Full credit courses?	NO	NO	NO	YES	NO	YES	NO
Lectures?	YES	YES	NO	YES	YES	YES	YES
B. A graduate program in special education that includes material on gifted/talented students?	NO	NO	NO	YES	NO	INO*	NO
A graduate program that offers courses on the education of gifted/talented students?	NO	NO	NO	NO	NO	YES	NO
C. Professional development activities for teachers of the gifted/talented?	YES	YES	NO	YES	YES	YES	NO

*Information not obtained

Appendix C:
School Boards that Submitted Supplementary Material

Respondents to the school board section of the CEA survey were invited to forward any material that they had produced in connection with a specific program for gifted and talented students. The material received from the school boards listed below included policy statements, parent information brochures, and descriptions of proposed programs.

BRITISH COLUMBIA

Chilliwack School District No. 33
Coquitlam School District No. 43
Kamloops School District No. 24
Nanaimo School District No. 68
Peace River South School District No. 59 (Dawson Creek)
Prince George School District No. 57
Saanich School District No. 63 (Sidney)
Vancouver School District No. 39, Teacher Centre
Vernon School District No. 22

ALBERTA

Calgary Board of Education
Edmonton Public School Board
Strathcona County Board of Education (Sherwood Park)

SASKATCHEWAN

Regina Roman Catholic Separate School Division No. 81
Regina School Division No. 4
Saskatoon (East) School Division No. 41

ONTARIO

Board of Education for the Borough of York (Toronto)
London and Middlesex County Roman Catholic Separate School Board (London)
Metropolitan Toronto Roman Catholic Separate School Board
Niagara South Board of Education (Welland)
Ottawa Board of Education
Scarborough Board of Education
Toronto Board of Education

QUÉBEC

Commission des écoles catholiques de Montréal
Commission scolaire Baldwin-Cartier (Pointe-Claire)
North Island Regional School Board* (City of Laval)

---

*This board has now joined with the Laval School Board to become the new Laurenval School Board.

Appendix D: Suggested Canadian Reading

All of the material in this list has been published in a magazine, book, or brochure, and therefore should be easily obtained.

Alexander, Betty. "The Gifted Child in the Kindergarten Classroom". *Venture Forth,* Vol. 7, No. 4 (Summer 1976), pp. 29-37.

Baker, V. Noreen, and D.H. Saklofske. "Guiding the Gifted Child in the Regular Elementary Classroom". *TASA* (Teaching Atypical Students in Alberta), Vol. 4, No. 1 (Fall 1974), pp. 24-34.

Banks, Ruth. "How Would You Like It If You Were Gifted?". *Special Education in Canada,* Vol. 53, No. 2 (Winter 1979), pp. 12-14.

Cassivi, Denis. "Special Programs for Gifted Children". *Journal of Education* (Nova Scotia), Vol. 5, No. 2 (Winter 1977-78), pp. 17-21.

Ertis, B.P.A. "Gilding the Gifted". *The Educational Courier,* Vol. 48, No. 2 (November 1977), pp. 14-17.

Folkman, Mel. "Providing for the Gifted and Talented". *The Intermediate Teacher,* Vol. 16, No. 2 (Fall 1976), pp. 37-40.

Gifted/Talented Children. Curriculum Ideas for Teachers series. Toronto: Ontario Ministry of Education, 1978.

Hawkes, C. "Help for the Egghead". *The Canadian Magazine,* 3 March 1979, pp. 6-8.

"How Not to Spot Gifted Children". Report of an address by Ken O'Bryan. *Reporter* (Ontario English Catholic Teachers' Association), Vol. 3, No. 3 (November 1977), p. 29.

O'Brien, Judy. "The 'Challenge' Program". *TASA,* Vol. 5, No. 1 (Fall 1975), pp. 39-43.

Orlik, H. "The Gifted Child". *Journal of Education* (N.S.), Vol. 4, No. 4 (Summer 1977), pp. 13-14.

Pace, Clare. "Counselling the Academically Bright". *The School Guidance Worker,* Vol. 32, No. 1 (September-October 1976), pp. 10-11.

Parker, Margaret. "What Can Be Learned from Brilliance in Children?". *Special Education in Canada,* Vol. 52, No. 1 (Fall 1977), pp. 19-21.

Sangster, C.H., and Georgina Adamson. "Nurturing Gifted Children". *Education Canada,* Vol. 17, No. 4 (Winter 1977), pp. 26-29.

Shiner, Sandra M. "Wanted: Gifted Teachers for Gifted Kids". *Orbit 41,* Vol. 9, No. 1 (February 1978), pp. 11-12.

Speed, Fred. "Teaching the Bright Child". *Orbit 41,* Vol. 9, No. 1 (February 1978), pp. 6-11.

Stephenson, Carolyn. "The Gifted Child: Reflections on his Place in School and in Society". *Orbit 23,* Vol. 5, No. 3 (June 1974), pp. 12-14.

Vernon, Philip E., Georgina Adamson, and Dorothy F. Vernon. *The Psychology and Education of Gifted Children.* London, Eng.: Methuen & Co., 1977.

Woodliffe, Helen M. "Education of the Gifted". *Orbit 41,* Vol. 9, No. 1 (February 1978), pp. 5-6.

Woodliffe, Helen M. *Teaching Gifted Learners: A Handbook for Teachers.* Profiles in Practical Education No. 11. Toronto: Ontario Institute for Studies in Education, 1977.

Ziv, Avner. "Guidance for the Gifted". *The School Guidance Worker,* Vol. 32, No. 1 (September-October 1976), pp. 45-47.